CONTENTS

England, from London to the North.

A BRIEF HISTORY OF

ROBIN HOOD

NIGEL CAWTHORNE

RUNNING PRESS
PHILADELPHIA · LONDON

ROBINSON

Constable & Robinson Ltd
3 The Lanchesters
162 Fulham Palace Road
London W6 9ER
www.constablerobinson.com

First published in the UK by Constable
an imprint of Constable & Robinson Ltd, 2010

A copy of the British Library Cataloguing in
Publication data is available from the British Library

UK ISBN: 978-1-84901-301-7

1 3 5 7 9 10 8 6 4 2

First published in the United States in 2010 by Running Press Book
Publishers

9 8 7 6 5 4 3 2 1
Digit on the right indicates the number of this printing

US ISBN 978-0-7624-3851-8

US Library of Congress Control Number: 2009935107

Running Press Book Publishers
2300 Chestnut Street
Philadelphia, PA 19103-4371

Visit us on the web!
www.runningpress.com

Printed and bound in the EU

Nigel Cawthorne has written numerous books on the myths and criminals of Britain. He lives in London. www.nigel-cawthorne.co.uk

Highlights from the Brief History/Brief Guide series

A Brief History of the Crusades
Geoffrey Hindley

A Brief History of the Druids
Peter Berresford Ellis

A Brief History of the Dynasties of China
Bamber Gascoigne

A Brief History of the Hundred Years War
Desmond Seward

A Brief History of the Private Lives of the Roman Emperors
Anthony Blond

A Brief History of Secret Societies
David V. Barrett

A Brief History of the Vikings
Jonathan Clements

A Brief History of the Universe
J P McEvoy

A Brief History of Middle East
Christopher Catherwood

A Brief History of the Kings and Queens of Britain
Mike Ashley

A Brief History of Henry VIII
Derek Wilson

A Brief History of Everyday Life in the Middle Ages
Martyn Whittock

A Brief History of Venice
Liz Horodowich

A Brief History of Mankind
Cyril Aydon

A Brief Guide to Greek Myths
Stephen Kershaw

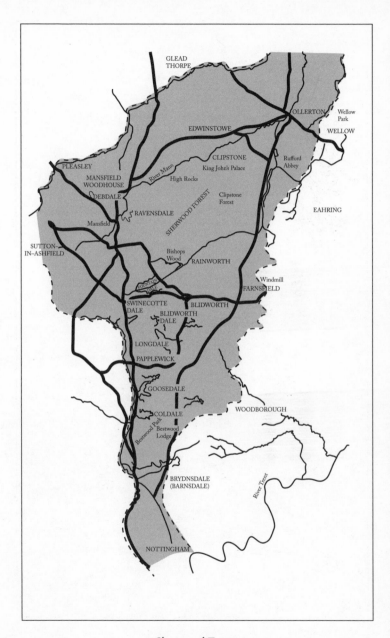

Sherwood Forest

INTRODUCTION

Some historians say that Robin Hood has no place in history, that he is a figure of myth made up by medieval balladeers. However, there are indications that such a person did exist and several real people may have contributed to the legend. There were undoubtedly a number of shady criminals inhabiting the forests of England in the Middle Ages who were called, or assumed the name of, Robin or Robert Hood, and a number of incidents in the tale of Robin Hood are borrowed from the lives of other outlaws of the time who are known to have been real.

A number of kings who are certainly historic figures are mentioned in various versions of the tale. Nottingham did have a sheriff – a series of them from 1068 on. There was a priory at Kirklees, where Robin is said to have died. And Little John, Friar Tuck and Will Scarlet can be linked to historical figures.

The story of Robin Hood also has a history of its own. In the earliest references, he appears to be merely a bandit, robbing travellers for his own survival or, perhaps, to enrich himself. But at the hands of the balladeers he is only interested in robbing those in authority, such as the sheriff or wealthy clerics. Those who were honest or poor were left largely unmolested.

Robin's major crime was poaching deer. This was seen as every freeborn Englishman's right, taken away from them by the Normans who brought the Forest Law with them from the Continent when they invaded in 1066. William the Conqueror himself was inordinately fond of hunting and cleared large areas of villagers and peasants to make way for the chase.

The *Anglo-Saxon Chronicle* says:

> whosoever slew a hart, or a hind should be deprived of his eyesight. As he [Willson] forbade men to kill the harts, so also the boars; and he loved the tall deer as if he were their father. Likewise he declared respecting the hares that they should go free. His rich bemoaned it, and the poor men shuddered at it.

One of the areas he cleared was the New Forest in Hampshire. Like other deer parks, it was policed by William's foresters who were employed to protect the game and anyone caught poaching was liable to lose their testicles as well as their eyes.

Things only got worse under William's son William Rufus (1087–1100) and Henry I (1100–35) who, it was said, had an 'army of evil men' to enforce the Forest Laws. And when Henry II (1154–89) became king, it was 'the custom for the royal foresters to be a complete law unto themselves, they put to death and mutilated whom they would without any trial whatever, or with but the mockery of the water-ordeal, a farce which had already been condemned by the church, but which was very fashionable with ruffians who were anxious to secure a conviction'.

Matters came to a head when foresters seized a priest with the intention of extorting money from him. The Bishop of Lincoln threatened them with excommunication and they let him go. Afterwards, the Forest Laws were administered with something more nearly approaching justice.

Even so, the feudal lord still had absolute power over his family. Robert de Belesme, Earl of Shropshire and of Arundel and Shrewsbury, one of the most powerful and defiant barons of Norman times, tore the eyes out of his own children when they hid their faces behind his cloak in a game. He had his wife locked in fetters and thrown into a dungeon, only to have his servants drag her to his bed each night and return her to gaol in the morning. This was done to extort money from her family, but it can hardly have promoted marital harmony. Not that that would have mattered to Robert de Belesme. He refused to ransom his captives, preferring to have both men and women impaled on stakes. Even his friends were a little wary; he could be chatting away one minute then suddenly plunge his sword into someone's side and laugh about it.

Robin and his Merry Men lived in these harsh times. In some of the ballads, they kill and maim without conscience. But, by and large, they embody the ideal of the stout yeoman, who drinks excessive amounts of ale and wine, and feasts on freshly killed venison.

The story of Robin Hood draws on history. It has had the feud between the Norman invaders and the Saxon inhabitants of old England thrust upon it. Prince John's attempt to usurp his brother's throne while Richard was away fighting in the crusades was added later. Some have seen in the tale the rebellion of Simon de Montfort in 1265 or that of Thomas, earl of Lancaster, against Edward II in 1322. There are also echoes of Hereward the Wake's stand against Norman rule in 1070–71 and William Wallace's resistance to English rule in Scotland in 1297–1305.

One piece of history can often be used to illuminate another. Shakespeare's *Henry V*, showing the English victory at Agincourt in 1415, took to the stage just ten years after the defeat of the Spanish Armada. In 1944, it took to the screen as a piece of propaganda in the Second World War. Earlier in the war, the film *That Hamilton Woman*, about the affair between Admiral Lord Nelson and Lady Hamilton, drew clear parallels between Britain being threatened by Hitler in 1941 and the country being threatened by Napoleon almost a century and a half before. Britain's Prime Minister Winston Churchill even wrote two of Nelson's speeches and the producer-director Alexander Korda was subpoenaed to appear before the US Senate committee on foreign relations to answer charges of 'inciting the American public to war', but the hearing was forestalled by the Japanese attack on Pearl Harbor which brought the United States into the war.

It is, perhaps, no accident that the classic Hollywood version *The Adventures of Robin Hood* came out in 1938, a year before the war in Europe started. At that time, Hollywood was full of European émigrés, fleeing Hitler. The director, Michael Curtiz, was a Hungarian Jew who later made *Casablanca*, another propaganda classic.

In the 1950s, the classic TV series, *The Adventures of Robin Hood*, was written by blacklisted Hollywood writers, some of whom were former communists. To them, the fact that Robin Hood robbed from the rich and gave to the poor had a particular appeal, along with his anti-authoritarian stand. They used it as a medium to criticize McCarthyite America.

In the early ballads, dating from the fourteenth century, Robin displays occasional bouts of generosity, but there is no reason to think that he gave his plunder away to the dispossessed. Nor is he a great hero. In the ballads, he is regularly bested in fights, but when he is about to get beaten he sounds his horn and is rescued by his Merry Men. He would then invite his opponent to join them.

Robin was not the greatest of archers either. Little John beat him in competitions – and Robin takes this badly. In early versions of the story, Little John appears to be the leader of the outlaws, rather than Robin – or at the very least co-leader. As the legend developed, he defers to Robin who gradually begins to show the qualities of a natural leader.

Robin Hood has been with us for some eight centuries now. From shadowy beginnings, he has developed through many incarnations. Each one is relevant to the time the tale is retold. And, no doubt, the tale of Robin Hood and his Merry Men will be retold many times in the future. Now that's history.

I

ROBIN HOOD AND HIS
MERRY MEN

Everyone knows Robin Hood. He was a famous outlaw and unrivalled archer living with his band of yeomen in Sherwood Forest, near the town of Nottingham, where they feasted on the King's venison washed down with warm English ale.

However, Robin was no outlaw by nature. When he was just eighteen, back in the reign of Henry II, the Sheriff of Nottingham organized an archery contest to find the best archer in Nottinghamshire – the prize, a butt of ale. In the nearby village of Locksley, Robin heard about this, picked up his bow and arrows and set off for Nottingham. On his way he passed through Sherwood Forest. It was a fine spring morning and Robin was thinking of his love Maid Marian, when he passed a bunch

of men, dressed in Lincoln green, eating pie and drinking
ale under a great oak tree. A little drunk, perhaps, they
taunted him about his 'penny bow and farthing arrows'.
Robin responded that his bow and arrows were as good as
theirs and they bet 20 marks (£13 6s 8d, or £13.33, a
massive sum in those days) that he could not hit a deer
threescore rods (330 yards or 301 metres) away. But when
he killed the deer they refused to pay up.

One of them offered to beat him up. Another pointed
out that he had killed one of the King's deer. The penalty
for that was to have your ears severed. When Robin made
off, one of the foresters fired an arrow at him. But the man
had been drinking. He missed. Robin turned and fired.
He hit his mark and killed the man. With that, he
disappeared into the forest. He had now become an
outlaw and, for poaching the King's deer, there was a price
of £200 on his head. The Sheriff of Nottingham swore to
bring him to justice, both to claim the £200 and because
the forester Robin had killed was a relative.

After a year in the forest, Robin had gathered around
him others like himself who had been outlawed by the
King, rich barons, abbots and squires. Robin was elected
their leader and they decided they would rob from the
rich, who had dispossessed them, and give to those
oppressed by heavy taxes, extortionate rents and wrongful
fines. They swore not to hurt women or children, lived in
huts made out of bark and slept on beds of rushes covered
with the skins of fallow deer.

One day, when Robin was crossing a narrow bridge,
he met a stranger coming from the other side. Neither
would give way. The man was seven foot tall – a head
and neck taller than Robin. Robin threatened him with
his bow and arrow, but the man called him a coward as

he was carrying nothing but a staff. To settle the matter, Robin cut himself a staff and the two of them fought. Though Robin landed a few blows, he was no match for the stranger and was knocked from the bridge into the stream below.

Robin's followers, the Merry Men, set upon the stranger, but Robin called them off. Instead he invited him to join them. The stranger refused, saying that if Robin handled a bow and arrow the way he handled a staff he was not fit to call himself a yeoman. Rising to the challenge once more, Robin got Will Stutely to cut a target four fingers wide and place it on an oak tree 80 yards (73 metres) away. The stranger fired an arrow, hitting the target dead centre and defied Robin to do better. When Robin fired, his arrow hit the shaft of his opponent's arrow, splitting it in two.

When the stranger was asked his name, he replied: 'John Little'. Over his objections, Will Stutely renamed him 'Little John'. He joined them in the forest where he was christened with ale and became Robin's right-hand man.

The Sheriff of Nottingham knew nothing of the band of outlaws Robin had gathered around him and issued a warrant for his arrest. Although he offered a fee of fourscore golden angels (some £53) no one would serve it. A messenger was set to Lincoln. On the way he stopped at the Blue Boar Inn where he met a tinker from Banbury who said he would serve the warrant. As the tinker was heading into Sherwood, he bumped into Robin but, as a stranger to the area, he did not recognize him. Together they went back to the Blue Boar, where the tinker got drunk. When he fell asleep, Robin stole the warrant and the fourscore angels. The tinker awoke to find that he could not pay for the ale they had drunk and had to leave his coat and tools as surety.

Heading out into the forest, the tinker bumped into Robin again. Determined to regain what he had lost – and take Robin to Nottingham to be hanged – the tinker challenged Robin to a fight. They fought with staves and Robin was winning when his staff broke. He blew on his horn and Little John and six of his Merry Men turned up. They threatened to hang the tinker. But, instead, Robin invited him to join them.

The King grew angry with the Sheriff of Nottingham for his failure to catch Robin Hood, so the Sheriff announced another archery contest. This time the prize would be an arrow of pure gold. Although they realized that this was a trap, Robin and the Merry Men were determined to go. They disguised themselves as friars, peasants, tinkers and beggars. Robin used walnut to dye his blonde hair and beard, dressed in tattered scarlet and wore a patch over one eye. He won the competition with an arrow that shaved the goose-feather flight off the Sheriff's man's arrow. The Sheriff said that he shot better than Robin Hood, who was a coward as he had not dared show his face at the competition. As he handed over the golden arrow, the Sheriff offered to take the prize-winning archer into his service, but Robin said that he was his own man and no man in Merry England would be his master.

Back in the greenwood, the Merry Men celebrated Robin's victory, but Robin was angry that the Sheriff had called him a coward. That night, while the Sheriff was feasting, an arrow came through the window and lodged in his table. Around the shaft was a note informing him that it was Robin Hood himself who had won the golden arrow.

The Sheriff then sent three hundred men out into Sherwood Forest. Their reward for capturing Robin dead or alive would be £100 – and £40 for one of his Merry Men. Robin refused to take them on. He had already killed one man and did not want to do it again, so he and his men hid out for seven days. But they had to know what the Sheriff's men were planning so Will Stutely was sent to the Blue Boar dressed as a friar. He was drinking with the Sheriff's men there, when a cat rubbed against his habit and they caught a glimpse of Lincoln green underneath. They jumped him. Stutely pulled out a broadsword, but they overpowered him and bound him hand and foot.

When Robin learnt that the Sheriff's men had taken Will Stutely to Nottingham to be hanged, he called his Merry Men together. The hanging was to take place in Nottingham in front of the Sheriff and the townsfolk. The Merry Men infiltrated the crowd. When one of the Sheriff's men-at-arms asked Little John to stand back, Little John felled him, grabbed the Sheriff's sword and gave it to Will Stutely. The rest of the Merry Men saw off the Sheriff's men-at-arms with swords and arrows. Together they fled back to the forest, leaving the Sheriff fearful as he had nearly lost his own life.

Robin hid out in Sherwood Forest for another year wondering how to get even with the Sheriff of Nottingham who had now tried to capture him three times. One day he ventured out of the forest and met a butcher. He bought the man's butcher's gown and his cartload of meat, which he sold overpriced to the rich and underpriced to the poor. One pretty woman paid with a kiss. That night the Sheriff of Nottingham was giving a feast for the butcher's guild. Disguised as a butcher, Robin was invited.

Over dinner Robin teased the Sheriff about giving the golden arrow to Robin Hood then, to make amends, he promised to use the money he had made from selling the meat to pay for the feast. He boasted that he owned so many acres of land that he could not count them and had at least five hundred head of livestock.

Seeking to take advantage of someone who seemed so careless with money, the Sheriff offered to buy the livestock for just £300, well below market price for cattle. The next day Robin took the Sheriff out of Nottingham to view them and complete the sale. As they rode into Sherwood Robin revealed that this was his vast estate and the livestock he was selling were the King's deer that grazed there. Robin and the Merry Men then laid on a feast for the Sheriff, seating him under the golden arrow. For entertainment, they put on displays of fencing and archery. Then Robin asked the Sheriff to pay for the feast, just as Robin himself had done the night before. When the Sheriff refused, he was introduced to Will Stutely and Little John. He handed over the £300. He left the forest with the laughter of the Merry Men ringing in his ears. Ballads soon circulated about how the Sheriff had gone out to shear, but had himself been shorn.

Every five years, a fair was held in Nottingham. As usual, there would be an archery competition. This time the prize would be two steers and a tun of ale. Robin did not think it worth going but, against Robin's advice, Little John went in disguise. He beat the local champion, Eric o' Lincoln, with the quarterstaff, then won the archery competition. Once more the Sheriff offered to take the victor into his service, saying he was second only to Robin Hood with the bow and arrow. Little John accepted the offer and gave his prize – the steers and ale – away to those at the fair.

Little John spent the winter in Nottingham Castle and became the Sheriff's right-hand man. But one spring morning, he lay in bed, thinking how much he missed his friends in the forest. Rising late, he was refused breakfast, so he punched a hole in the pantry door and helped himself. When the steward upbraided him, he knocked him out. The cook was then sent to fight Little John, but thought better of it and joined Little John in a feast. The two of them got drunk on the Sheriff's sack and canary wine, and sang ballads. That done, they decided that they had better finish the fight and drew their swords. The sword fight prove indecisive and, during a rest, Little John persuaded the cook to join him and the Merry Men in Sherwood for the usual fee – two suits of Lincoln green and 40 marks (£26 13s 4d) a year. They took with them as much of the Sheriff's silverware as they could carry.

Robin welcomed Little John back, but was angry with them for stealing the silver as they had enough trouble with the Sheriff already. Little John protested that they had been given the silverware; he would go and fetch the Sheriff to confirm it. He found the Sheriff out hunting and told him that he had seen a young buck and a herd of deer that were green from head to toe. The Sheriff said he was mad, but Little John told him to follow him into the forest where he could see for himself. Then Little John led him to Robin Hood, saying 'Yonder is the hart of which I spake.'

Robin then offered the Sheriff wine in one of his own silver flagons. When he refused it, Robin asked him whether he did not like their new silver service. Then

Robin relented. He returned the Sheriff's silver to him and led him out of the forest, saying that, as he had not come to do any harm, he would not take a farthing from him on that occasion.

Soon after Robin sent Little John to buy Lincoln green from the draper Hugh Longshanks of Ancaster, giving him a bag of gold from the outlaws' treasure house, which was locked in a cave behind stout wooden doors. But, instead of going straight to Ancaster, Little John stopped off in the Blue Boar Inn. The following morning, he got into a fight with a tanner named Arthur á Bland but, as he had grown soft and fat from living at the Sheriff's, Little John was beaten. Robin, who had heard that Little John had stopped off at the Blue Boar, caught up with him in time to see the fight and asked the tanner to join the Merry Men.

Further down the road they saw a pretty, mincing lad, dressed in scarlet silk, with blonde hair that fell in curls to his shoulders. On his head he wore scarlet velvet with a long feather in it and in his hand he carried a rose. Little John dismissed him as a 'rose-leaf and whipped-cream gallant'. Robin agreed that the lad left a nasty taste in his mouth, but decided that he must be a baron's son with a rich purse. Thinking that he was a Norman, Robin was determined to rob him. Little John pointed out that Normans had dark hair. Robin asked when he had seen a Saxon mince like that – but if he was a Saxon they would let the lad go without stealing from him.

Robin stopped the stranger and asked him to hand over his purse as a tithe to make candlesticks for the shrine of St Wilfred, threatening that those 'fat from overliving must needs lose blood'. The stranger drew a sword. Robin advised him that a sword was no match for an oak staff, but instead of cutting one the fey stranger pulled up a small tree by the roots. Little John was impressed.

After a long fight, Robin was knocked down and forced to yield. Little John then stepped in. The stranger threatened to take on both of them, but Robin had had enough and asked the stranger his name. He said it was Will Gamwell. He came from Maxfield town in search of his mother's young brother, Robin Hood. Robin introduced himself, and the young man explained that he was an outlaw. He had hit a man who had insulted his father and killed him. So he was now seeking refuge with his uncle. Robin welcomed him with open arms. For his gay attire, Robin and his Merry Men christened the new recruit Will Scarlet and they set off back to Sherwood Forest.

Stopping for lunch of bread and cheese, they drank some ale and took to singing ballads about King Arthur. Then they spotted a miller coming down the road, carrying a heavy sack, and decided to play a joke on him. They pretended to be common thieves. But when they tried to take his sack, he warned them that he was an honest tradesman who was safe from thieves on Robin Hood's territory.

'I fear Robin Hood no more than I do myself,' said Robin.

The miller said that he had no money, but when they threatened to turn out the flour on the ground he said there was gold and silver under it. Then he pretended to look for bullion in the sack. Suddenly, he pulled out two handfuls of flour and threw it in their faces and, while they were blinded, set about them with a staff. Robin begged him to stop, saying that he was Robin Hood. But the miller said Robin Hood would not have tried to rob an honest tradesman. Then Robin found his horn and blew it. Will Stutely and David of Doncaster arrived to find them white from head to toe, fighting it out in the middle of the road. They eventually restrained the miller and Robin invited him to join the Merry Men.

Two days later, Robin sent Will Stutely, the tanner and the miller out to invite someone to dine with them, so they could rob him. But all they met were damsels, milkmaids, shepherds, farmers and honest tinkers; no fat abbots, rich squires or money-lenders. Then they found a minstrel asleep under a tree with a harp of polished wood inlaid with gold and silver hanging from its branches.

Deep in the forest the minstrel, whose name was Allan á Dale, apologized to Robin that he had no money, only half a sixpence hung around his neck on a silken threat. The other half he had given to his true love, whose name was Ellen. But when her father had discovered they were lovers he given the damsel in marriage to an old and wealthy knight, Sir Stephen of Trent. The wedding was in two days' time.

Robin said that Allan á Dale would marry his true love, but they would need a compliant clergyman who was not afraid of an abbot or bishop. Will Scarlet said he knew of a such friar at Fountain Abbey, which was half a day's walk away. He would perform the service if there was food and drink involved. This was, of course, Friar Tuck. Allan á Dale then sang a song about his true love and Robin invited him to join the Merry Men.

The next day, Robin set out for Fountain Abbey. On the way, he met a friar carousing by the side of a stream. Robin was wearing a fine coat of chain mail which he did not want to get wet in the stream and persuaded the friar to carry him across. The friar also carried Robin's sword, but refused to give it back until Robin had promised to return the favour and carry the friar back across the stream. On the way, Robin unbuckled the friar's belt. Reaching the other side, Robin seized the friar's sword and refused to return it until the friar carried him back to the further bank again. But halfway across, the friar heaved Robin into the water. They then had a sword fight that lasted for an hour. Eventually Robin sounded his horn and his followers appeared. So the friar blew a whistle, summoning four ferocious dogs. The Merry Men fired arrows at the dogs who, miraculously, evaded them. But Will Scarlet stepped forward and pacified them as he knew the friar and his dogs. He then introduced Robin to Friar Tuck.

After a hard night's drinking in Sherwood Forest, Friar Tuck hid in the church where Ellen's wedding to Sir Stephen was to take place. Meanwhile Robin, dressed as a minstrel, waylaid Sir Stephen's brother, the richly attired Bishop of Hereford, and promised to play a tune that would make the bride love the man she married. So Robin was invited to the wedding, but during the ceremony Robin intervened, saying that the knight was too old to marry such a young lass and that he was not her true love. He sounded his horn and the Merry Men appeared and subdued Sir Stephen's men-at-arms. Then Friar Tuck emerged to read the banns and marry Ellen to Alan á Dale. Robin gave her father 200 gold angels as a dowry.

Robin turned to the bishop and said that he had fulfilled his promise – he had played his tune and the bride was in love with her husband. Then he asked the bishop to hand over the gold chain he wore around his neck and gave it to Ellen as a wedding present. Robin then invited the bishop to be their guest in Sherwood Forest.

Meanwhile, Friar Tuck asked whether the Merry Men needed someone to attend to religious matters and Robin invited him to join them.

Robin and his Merry Men regularly scoured the countryside for wealthy travellers who they would invite to feast with them – then demand the reckoning. One day Robin came across a sorrowful knight who looked a likely mark. But, when challenged, Sir Richard of Lea swore on his honour as a knight that he only had ten shillings in his purse – and in the world. His estates had been pawned to the Priory of Emmet against £500 he had borrowed to keep his son out of jail after he had accidentally killed a nobleman at a joust. If he did not pay back the loan in three days his estates would be lost forever. After a feast in the forest with the Bishop of Hereford, who they were still holding, Robin gave the sorrowful knight the money to redeem his estates in the form of the gold coin they had stolen from the bishop. Ashamed to see a knight in such a sorrowful state, they also gave him gold chains, gold spurs and rolls of velvet, along with gold cloth for his lady, and provided him with an escort. The bishop was only released three days later after his money had been paid to the Priory of Emmet.

When Sir Richard turned up to pay off his debt, the Prior was boasting to the Sheriff of Nottingham that he would soon own the noblest estate in Derbyshire for a mere £500. The knight then acted the supplicant and begged for his debt to be forgiven as an act of Christian charity. Thinking Sir Richard penniless, the prior taunted him, saying that he could redeem the debt for a mere £300. With that Sir Richard produced the bishop's gold. He paid over the £300, which the Prior was forced to accept as the knight was accompanied by Little John and the Merry

Men. Sir Richard used the rest of the money to renovate his castle and estates. A year later, he went to repay the money to Robin. On the way, he rescued one of Robin's men, David of Doncaster, who had been set upon after a wrestling match. Robin refused payment, but Sir Richard insisted. He also gave each man a bow and a quiver full of arrows. Robin's bow and quiver were inlaid with gold.

In search of adventure, Little John decided to take to the road as a strolling friar, while Robin would roam the country as a beggar. On the road to Tuxford, Little John met three pretty damsels taking eggs to market. He carried their baskets for them and, even though he was dressed as a friar, took a kiss from each in payment. While drinking and singing profane songs at an inn, Little John met two real friars. Further down the road, he begged them for money to buy a crust of bread. When they said they had no money, he forced them to get down from their horses, kneel in the road and pray to St Dunstan. He then prayed that St Dunstan give them ten shillings each. Then he looked in their pouches and found they had £40. He left them a pound – 20 shillings – as that was the answer to his prayer. The rest, he reasoned, belonged to him and he returned with it to Sherwood.

Meanwhile Robin came upon a beggar who was laden with stolen food. Robin bought some ale and they shared the feast. Robin then offered the beggar two gold angels if he would change clothes with him so he could learn his craft. The beggar took umbrage and a fight ensued. It ended when Robin knocked the beggar down. He then consented to give Robin his clothes, provided he took nothing else from him. When Robin agreed, the beggar cut open the lining of his coat and took out ten gold sovereigns hidden there. Then they changed clothes and parted.

Further down the road, Robin came upon four beggars having a feast on the ground. They each wore a sign around their neck saying they were 'deaf', 'blind', 'dumb' or 'lame'.

The deaf one was the first to hear Robin coming. The blind one was the first to see him. The dumb one called out for him to join then, while the lame man unstrapped his wooden leg and stretched his real leg out on the grass. Robin took the flask of Malmsey wine they offered and drank to their happiness; there was no point in drinking to their health as they were hale in wind and limb.

The 'blind' beggar asked him where he had some from. Robin said Sherwood. The beggars then said that, with all the money they were carrying, they would not stop in Sherwood for fear of Robin Hood. But when Robin showed his ignorance of the beggars' jargon, they accused him of being a spy. They attacked him. He knocked down the blind man and the dumb man, while the deaf man and the lame man fled. The blind man was carrying £200 in gold, which Robin took, along with the flask of Malmsey.

On his way back to Sherwood, Robin met an infamous corn merchant from Worksop who had once bought up all the grain in the district, only selling it when prices soared causing a famine. Robin asked him for a farthing to buy bread. The man refused, saying that even if Robin Hood was to search him, he would find nothing. Robin then confided that, despite appearances, he was not a beggar. He was a wealthy merchant. To prove it, he showed him the money he had stolen from the beggars and asked the corn merchant to accompany him to Newark. Along the way, the merchant, now trusting his companion, revealed that he was carrying £180 hidden in the soles of his clogs. Robin then said he would go no further as he had friends who lived nearby. The merchant should go on alone – barefoot. The merchant protested. Robin revealed he was Robin Hood and the man took off his clogs without further ado. Apologizing for not inviting the merchant to feast in the forest, Robin sent him on his way. That night Robin and Little John swapped stories over the campfire.

Eleanor of Aquitaine, wife of Henry II, sent for Robin. His presence was required at an archery contest in Finsbury Fields. Robin agreed to go, taking Little John, Will Scarlet and Allan á Dale with him. Four days later, they were in London Town. The queen laid on a feast for Robin and asked him about the Bishop of Hereford and Sir Richard of Lea.

There were eight hundred entrants to the archery contest. First prize was 90 gold sovereigns, a silver bugle inlaid with gold and a quiver with ten white arrows with gold tips and swan-feather flights. Second prize was a hundred fat bucks, and third prize was two tuns of Rhein wine. Each finalist would be given 80 silver pennies for taking part.

As the field was whittled down, Eleanor had a side bet with the King. If her men won, they would be given a free pardon for forty days. The King agreed. Robin Hood, Little John, Will Scarlet and Allan á Dale then stepped forward. The Bishop of Hereford recognized them immediately, but the King said he had already given his word. If they won, they would receive a pardon – but they had better watch out after the forty days were up.

Even though they were up against the King's finest archers, Robin and his men won a convincing victory and the King left the tournament fuming. The Bishop of

Hereford warned that, once Robin Hood returned to the woodland, he would be beyond the law forever. So the King sent six yeomen of the guard to seize him. But the Queen had already warned Robin that the King intended to break his word. By the time the yeomen reached Finsbury Fields, Robin and his men were already on their way back to the Midlands.

They stopped for the night at an inn in Barnet, where they ate and drank sack, and Little John flirted with the barmaid. Before they had finished the Queen's page arrived to warn Robin that the King had sent a hundred men to prevent him returning to safety in the woodlands; two companies of horse were not far behind.

Robin told his men that they were heading for St Albans, but just outside Barnet they split up. Robin went west; the other three east. They were to avoid the highways until they got back to Sherwood. Meanwhile the landlord of the inn, who had overheard the conversation, told the King's horsemen they were heading for St Albans and the soldiers rode off northwards on a wild-goose chase.

Once he heard that Robin had slipped through the net, the Bishop of Hereford rode to Nottingham, where he and the Sheriff sent out their men to block all roads to the south, west and east of Sherwood.

It took Little John, Will Scarlet and Allan á Dale eight days to reach Sherwood. They travelled via Chelmsford, Cambridge and Lincolnshire, and approached Sherwood from the north. They met none of the King's men along the way. Robin travelled through Aylesbury, Woodstock in Oxfordshire and Warwick. After seven days, he reached Dudley in Staffordshire. Thinking he had travelled far enough north, he turned eastwards through

Litchfield and Ashby-de-la-Zouch. Then he headed for Stanton. From there, he could smell the woodlands.

A little further on, Robin bent down to drink from a stream when an arrow whistled passed his ear. He leapt to his feet. As he dived into a thicket six more arrows followed him. One of them pierced his doublet, but did not penetrate the steel coat underneath.

The King's men leapt from their horses and chased after him into the thicket. But Robin knew the lay of the land better then they did and soon left them behind. Spotting another band of the King's men three miles further on, he kept on running until he reached Mackworth, just outside Derby. There, he stopped for a rest under a hedge. He was hungry and thirsty, and he prayed to St Dunstan for food and drink. A cobbler called Quince came by carrying a boiled capon and a pottle – half a gallon – of ale. Robin knew him to be rather thick. When he asked what Robin was doing under a hedge, Robin told Quince that he was catching gold birds by putting salt made from moonbeams on their tails and offered ten shillings to change clothes with him. That done, they ate the capon and washed it down with ale. They were just having a sing-song when six horsemen turned up and grabbed Quince, mistaking him for Robin whose clothes he was now wearing. Though Robin protested, Quince was flattered to be mistaken for the famous outlaw and confessed. So the horsemen bound his hands and took him to the Bishop of Hereford to claim their reward.

Robin headed on towards Sherwood but, exhausted by a journey of over 140 miles, he stopped at an inn just 5 miles outside Nottingham. As he slept, a friar from Emmet Priory took shelter from a thunderstorm in the inn. He asked for a bed for the night and was not best pleased when he was told he would have to share with a cobbler.

When Robin awoke in the morning, he saw the friar's habit hanging up and swapped it for the cobbler's clothes. He then made off with the friar's mule and his purse with ten gold sovereigns in it. When he awoke, the friar had no choice but to don the cobbler's clothes. Quince had now been found out and, a little way down the road, the friar was seized by the King's men on suspicion of being Robin Hood.

Robin was nearing Sherwood when he met Sir Richard of Lea, who warned him that the Sheriff's men were stopping everyone. Sir Richard said Robin must go back to London and seek the protection of the Queen. Dressing him as a retainer, they headed for London.

Queen Eleanor was walking in the royal gardens when Robin leaped over the walk and knelt at her feet. He threw herself on her mercy. The Queen then went to see the King, whose temper had now subsided. He renewed his promise of a pardon and gave Robin his head page to escort him back to Sherwood. Soon after, King Henry died and his son Richard I – Richard the Lion-Heart – inherited the throne.

Out in Sherwood, Robin met a stranger dressed in hide, armed with a bow and arrow, a broadsword and a double-edged dagger. He announced that he was Guy of Gisborne. He was an outlaw sent by the Bishop of Hereford to the Sheriff of Nottingham, who said he would give him a free pardon if he hunted down Robin Hood and brought him in dead or alive.

Robin had heard of Guy of Gisborne and the murderous deeds he had done in Herefordshire, but Gisborne did not recognize Robin. Highhandedly,

Gisborne dismissed the famous Robin Hood as a threat as he had killed no one, except when he had first come to the forest. Robin protested that Gisborne's quarry was a great archer and Gisborne, eager to demonstrate his prowess with the bow, challenged him to a contest.

Robin cut a stick twice the thickness of a man's thumb, shaved off the bark and set it up in front of an oak tree 80 paces away. Gisborne said that not even the devil could hit that. Robin agreed when Gisborne missed it twice. Then, with his second shot, Robin split it in two.

'I am Robin Hood,' he announced, drawing his sword.

Gisbourne told Robin to make his Confession and he too drew his sword. There followed a furious swordfight. More than once the point of Gisborne's sword pierced Robin's flesh and drops of blood fell upon the ground. Leaping back from another thrust, Robin's heel caught on a root and he fell on his back. Gisborne went in for the kill, but Robin grabbed the blade of his sword. Though it cut the palm of his hand, he parried the thrust so the sword buried its blade deep into the ground. Robin then leaped to his feet and slashed Gisborne under the sword arm. He let go of the sword, leaving it embedded in the ground. Robin then closed in. Before Gisborne could regain his balance, he thrust his sword through his heart and killed him. Robin put on Gisborne's clothes, pulled the hood over his head and rode into Nottingham looking for the Sheriff.

Meanwhile, Little John came across a widow whose three sons had just been arrested for killing a deer. They had been taken to the Sheriff of Nottingham, who was at the King's Head, an inn a mile from Nottingham on the southern border of Sherwood Forest. The Sheriff laughed at their pleas for mercy and ordered them to be hanged.

Little John turned up disguised as peasant and the Sheriff offered him sixpence – tuppence a head – to string up the three boys. Little John accepted.

As he put the nooses around their necks, he slyly cut the bonds around their wrists, but whispered to them not to flee until he gave the signal. Little John then asked the Sheriff if he could notch an arrow in his bow so he could shoot the young men in the heart to spare them a long and painful death. The Sheriff gave his permission. Once the arrow was in the bow, Little John shouted: 'Run'. The three boys pulled the nooses from their necks and raced for the safety of the woods.

Meanwhile, Little John turned the bow and arrow on the Sheriff's men, warning if any approached they would die. Then he backed slowly into the forest. Before he reached it, the Sheriff spurred his horse to ride him down. Little John pulled back his bowstring, but before he could loose the arrow the bow splintered. The Sheriff swung his sword and struck Little John with the flat of it, knocking him out.

Little John woke up sitting back-to-front on a horse, about to be strung up, when one of the Sheriff's men announced that Guy of Gisborne was approaching. His heart sank. Not only were the man's clothes covered in blood, he was carrying Robin's bugle, his broadsword and his bow. Robin was surely dead.

The man approaching announced that he had killed the vilest outlaw who had ever entered the forest. Little John cursed him. He then asked the Sheriff that, as he had killed the master, might he not also kill his knave, stuck like a porker up against a tree. The Sheriff ordered Little John to be taken down from the horse and stood against a tree with his hands still bound. Robin then put his bow, horn and broadsword on the ground near the tree and asked the Sheriff's men to stand back. With a deft slash of Guy of Gisborne's knife, he cut the rope around Little John's wrists. Robin notched an arrow in Gisborne's bow and held the Sheriff and his men back, while Little John grabbed Robin's weapons. He put the bugle to his lips and blew.

The Sheriff of Nottingham now saw Robin's face under Gisborne's hood and galloped off, followed by his men. The Merry Men sprung from the undergrowth. Little John loosed off an arrow which stuck out of the Sheriff's backside like a tail feather as he raced through the gates of Nottingham. For a month he had to sit on the softest cushions.

Two months later, King Richard was on a royal progress through England and stopped at Nottingham. As the Sheriff rode into the city accompanying the King, he saw in the crowd the faces of Robin Hood, Little John, Will Scarlet, Allan á Dale, Will Stutely, Friar Tuck and the other Merry Men. He blanched. The King thought he was ill.

At evening at a great feast in the Guild Hall, the King asked the Sheriff of Nottingham to tell him about Robin Hood. The Sheriff said he was a common outlaw, but Sir Richard of Lea's son Henry, who had been with the King in Palestine, told the King how Robin had saved his father's estate. The King said he would freely give £100 if he could meet Robin and was told that it could be arranged.

The next day Richard donned the robes of the Order of the Black Friars, with a purse containing £100 under it, and with his cowl up rode out of Nottingham. As soon as he entered Sherwood Forest, he was stopped by Robin, who took him to be a rich friar. He ordered Richard to hand over his purse. Will Scarlet counted the contents, took £50 and landed the other £50 back. Robin led the friar into the forest to feast with his Merry Men. Although Robin was still unaware who his latest dinner guest was, he proposed a toast to King Richard. The Merry Men then put on a display of archery and wrestling. Richard challenged Robin, wagering the £50 that had been returned to him. He then knocked Robin down and won back the other £50.

Then Sir Richard of Lea turned up, warning Robin that King Richard had left Nottingham looking for him, and offered to hide him in Castle Lea. It was then he was introduced to the tall friar, who he instantly recognized. The King threw back his cowl and everyone fell to their knees.

The King wanted to know why Sir Richard was seeking to protect a known thief against the King's law. Then Henry, Sir Richard's son, who had been part of Richard's escort, threw back his cowl too. Although he had served the King loyally in Palestine, he said that he would also offer his protection to a noble outlaw like Robin. The King praised him for speaking so boldly and announced a pardon for Robin Hood and all his Merry Men. But they could not continue to roam the forest; Robin, Little John, Will Scarlet and Allan á Dale were to come with him to London. The other Merry Men would be employed as forest rangers whose job would be to look after the King's deer.

The King slept in the forest that night. The following morning he rode into Nottingham with Robin Hood and his Merry Men, then on to London. Little John became champion of all England with the quarterstaff before returning to Nottinghamshire. Will Scarlet returned to inherit his father's lands. Robin was made Earl of Huntingdon and followed the King to war. Allan á Dale, along with his wife Ellen, followed Robin to immortalize his life in ballads.

After Richard I died on the battlefield in France, Robin returned to England and asked King John to give him leave to visit Nottingham. This was granted, but the new King told him he could not stay any longer than three days in Sherwood. In Nottingham, Robin and Allan á Dale avoided the Sheriff and rode out into the forest. There Robin sounded his bugle. By chance, Little John was within earshot and came running. Then Will Stutely and other Merry Men arrived. In front of them all, Robin said that he was renouncing the name Robert, Earl of Huntingdon, and resuming the nobler title of Robin Hood, the Yeoman.

The news got back to King John who took affront. He sent Sir William Dale with an army to bring back Robin dead or alive. In Nottingham Sir William then authorized the Sheriff to raise more men to hunt down Robin. Once again, Robin Hood proved elusive. Finally, the forces of the crown caught up with the Merry Men. The first man killed in the ensuing melee was the Sheriff of Nottingham, shot in the head with an arrow. Sir William was wounded and most of his men slaughtered.

Robin was disturbed by this butchery and came down with fever. Little John took him to the Nunnery of Kirklees, where Robin's cousin the Prioress would look after him. Fearing King John would turn against her, the Prioress locked Robin in a room and began to bleed him daily until his life began to ebb away. With the last of his strength, he sounded his horn. Little John heard it, broke into the room and forced the Prioress to staunch the bleeding. But it was clear he was dying.

Robin got Little John to raise him up so that he could see the woodland one last time. Then he asked for a bow and arrow. He fired the arrow out of the window and told Little John that he was to be buried where it had fallen. The spot was to be kept ever green and his bones were not to be disturbed. That night Robin Hood died.

That is a summary of the standard version of the story. But this tale is not from the twelfth century, when the story is set. Nor is it English. It comes from the American writer Howard Pyle who published his *The Merry Adventures of Robin Hood of Great Renown in Nottinghamshire* in 1883. He also produced the illustrations that have been used as the foundation of our images of Robin Hood.

Pyle's story, although created nearly 700 years after the supposed events, is compiled from the stories in earlier ballads. However, there may have been a real Robin Hood living in the late twelfth century, or thereabouts. The *Oxford Dictionary of National Biography*, the authoritative tome which contains the life stories of anyone who has done anything in British history, has a long entry on Robin Hood.

2

THE BIRTH OF THE LEGEND

The tale of Robin Hood has been retold so many times between its inception and 1883 that it can be viewed as merely a literary invention. However, a real figure can be glimpsed through the mists of time. If he is a fictional character he is not a recent one. In William Langland's narrative poem *The Vision of Piers Plowman*, written around 1377, Sloth, the lazy priest, says that, while he does not know the Lord's Prayer, he does know 'rhymes of Robin Hood and Randolf, earl of Chester'. This indicates that tales of Robin Hood had already been around long enough to have appeared in poems and ballads. Geoffrey Chaucer also makes a reference to the 'haselwode, there joly Robyn played' in his poem *Troilus and Criseyde*, written in the 1380s. And in an edition of the *Canterbury Tales* from around 1460–80 Robin Hood was substituted for Bevis of Hampton in 'The Tale of Sir Thopas' and mentions 'sir By'.

Langland's poem is set in the Malvern Hills, where Langland himself was thought to have been born, though references in the poem suggest that he was also familiar with London, Westminster and Shropshire. So the rhymes of Robin Hood had been around long enough to spread far outside Nottinghamshire – or Yorkshire, another county that lays claim to Robin Hood.

The coupling of Robin Hood and Randolf, earl of Chester suggests that they lived around the same time. Before the publication of Dr Johnson's dictionary in 1755, English spelling was notoriously malleable and the most likely candidate for Langland's Randolf, earl of Chester, seems to be the third and last Ranulf, earl of Chester. Born in 1170, he came to prominence in the court of Henry II and was knighted by the King on 1 January 1189, according to the Chester annals. He was then charged with resisting the French invasion of Brittany. Henry II (1154–89) of England was also duke of Normandy, duke of Aquitaine and count of Anjou – his 'Angevin Empire' extended from Scotland to the Pyrenees. With Henry's death in July 1189, Ranulf moved out of the limelight. He did not accompany Henry's son Richard I (1189–99) on the Third Crusade. However, in 1194, he helped Richard retake Nottingham Castle, the last garrison of John, his brother who had tried to usurp the throne while Richard was held in captivity in Austria on his way home from the Holy Land.

When Richard died in 1199, Ranulf supported John's claim to the throne over that of Richard's chosen successor, Ranulf's stepson Arthur of Brittany. This ended Ranulf's marriage to Arthur's mother Constance, who

Ranulf long kept imprisoned in the castle of St Jacques de Beurvon in Normandy. Although Ranulf was often in disfavour with the King, he remained loyal to John, initially siding with him against the barons before John was forced to sign Magna Carta. Afterwards, Ranulf issued his own Magna Carta of Cheshire, defining local customs, and received substantial rewards from John.

When John died, Ranulf swore allegiance to John's son Henry III, who was nine. Ranulf raised an army to attack Mountsorrel Castle near Leicester and fought at the battle of Lincoln, expelling Prince Louis of France – later Louis VIII (1223–6) – who also claimed the throne of England. As a reward he was made first earl of Lincoln as well as sixth earl of Chester and vicomte of Bessin and Avranchin on the Norman–Breton frontier. In 1218, Ranulf joined the Fifth Crusade. After he returned to England in 1220, he was frequently at odds with the government, though he fought for the King again in France in 1230–31. He died at Wallingford in 1232. His heart was buried at Dieulacres Abbey in Staffordshire, which he had refounded in 1214, and his body was interred at St Werburgh's Abbey in Chester. Living from 1170 to 1232, Ranulf, earl of Chester, was around in the same troubled period in which Robin Hood was supposed to have lived.

The tale of Robin Hood then moves to Scotland. By 1420 Andrew Wyntoun, the prior of St Serf's in Lochleven, had completed a rhyming chronicle of Scotland up to 1408, called the *Original Chronicle of Scotland*. Under the years 1283–5, he wrote: 'Litil Johun and Robert Hude, Waythmen war commendit gud; In Yngilwode and Bernnysdaile, Thai oysyd all this time thar travail' – that is, 'Little John and Robin Hood were well praised forest outlaws; all this time they did their deeds in Inglewood and Barnsdale'. At that time Robin was a familiar diminutive of Robert. 'Waythmen' were ambushers who laid in wait and Inglewood means 'English wood'. Although there is no indication where he got his information from, Wyntoun would have heard the same rhymes that William Langland referred to.

The order of the names is interesting too. Robin may have followed Little John to make the rhyme with 'good', but it also implies that Little John was the leader of the outlaw band – or, at least, they were co-leaders. And Wyntoun does not set their deeds in Sherwood Forest of Nottinghamshire, but further north in Inglewood, the 'English wood' south of Carlisle, and in Barnsdale. There is a Barnsdale Forest in south Yorkshire where other sources place Robin Hood. However, there is also a Barnsdale Forest in the county of Rutland, twenty-five miles southeast of Nottingham. In it, there is a Robin Hood's Field and a Robin Hood's Cave, and nearby a Robin Hood's Cross. In the vicinity there are also two topographic references to Little John. The area was long associated with outlaws. An estate in the forest was owned by the earl of Huntington, a title held by the Scots Royal Family. The Scottish king also retained six estates in Inglewood when he gave up his claim to Cumberland and Westmoreland in the reign of Henry III (1216–72). Wyntoun dates his Robin Hood and Little John to 1283–5, the decade before the 'Braveheart' rebellion of William Wallace in Scotland. He seems to be implying that even good Englishmen rebelled against their oppressive king. It should also be remembered that after their defeat at the battles of Dunbar in 1296 and Falkirk in 1298, Wallace and his men took to the forests like the legendary outlaw.

There were other mentions of Robin Hood around Barnsdale, Yorkshire. The cartulary, or register, of Monk Bretton Priory near Barnsley in south Yorkshire mentions a stone of Robin Hood near Slephill in Barnsdale around 1422. And the Court of Common Pleas recorded that 'Robin Hode in Barnsdale stode' in 1429.

In the 1440s, another Scotsman Walter Bower was writing his *Scotichronicon*, an expansion of an earlier work by John of Fordun. Under the year 1266, Bower added:

Then arose the famous cutthroat, Robert Hood, as well as Little John, together with their accomplices from among the dispossessed, whom the foolish populace are so inordinately fond of celebrating both in tragedy and comedy, and about whom they are delighted to hear the jesters and minstrels sing above all other ballads. About whom also certain praiseworthy things are told, as appears in this – that when once in Barnsdale, avoiding the anger of the King and the threats of the prince, he was according to his custom most devoutly hearing Mass and had no wish on any account to interrupt the service – on a certain day, when he was hearing Mass, having been discovered in that very secluded place in the woods when the Mass was taking place by a certain viscount [sheriff] and servant of the King, who had very often lain in wait for him previously, there came to him those who had found this out from their men to suggest that he should make every effort to flee. This, on account of his reverence for the sacrament in which he was then devoutly involved, he completely refused to do. But, the rest of his men trembling through fear of death, Robert, trusting in the one so great who he worshipped, with the few who then bravely remained with him, confronted his enemies and easily overcame them, and enriched by the spoils he took from them and their ransom, ever afterwards singled out the servants of the church and the Masses to be held in greater respect, bearing in mind what is commonly said: 'God harkens to him who hear Mass frequently.'

Placing Robin in 1266 would have put him among the dispossessed followers of Simon de Montfort – cousin of Ranulf, earl of Chester – who rebelled against Henry III in 1264. Ruling in Henry's place, de Montfort sought to give his government some sort of legitimacy by calling a parliament of representatives of the boroughs and shires. This is the basis of the modern British parliament. However, de Montfort was defeated and killed at the battle of Evesham in August 1265 by Henry's son Prince Edward, later Edward I (1272–1307). This chimes nicely with the idea of Robin Hood as proto-democrat, fighting for the rights of the people. Bower also makes Robin a devout Christian. Deep in the forest, he celebrates Mass, refusing to be disturbed by a marauding 'viscount' or sheriff. He then goes on to rout his enemy.

However, there was another desperado on the run at the time. After the battle of Evesham, one of de Montfort's followers, Roger Godberd, was outlawed. In September 1266, he had descended on Garendon abbey, demanding the land that the abbot and monks had leased from him and bonds they had for money he owed them. He held out in Sherwood Forest and, with a band of up to a hundred men, terrorized Nottinghamshire, Derbyshire and Leicester. The King wrote to Roger Leland, constable of Nottingham, giving his permission to the townsfolk to take timber from the royal forest to fortify the city's defences. In 1272, Godberd was captured by Reginald de

Grey, one-time Sheriff of Nottingham and a former comrade in arms of Godberd's who had undertaken the task as a special commission for the payment of one hundred marks. The King's letter to Grey spells out the extent of Godberd's criminal activities:

> Through outlaws, robbers, thieves and malefactors, mounted and on foot . . . wandering by day and night, so many and great homicides and robberies were done that no one with a small company could pass through those parts without being taken and killed or spoiled of his goods . . . and no religious or other persons could pass without being taken and spoiled of his goods.

Richard Foliot, a local knight, was accused of harbouring Godberd, inviting the parallel with Sir Richard of the Lea, or Syr Richard at the Lee as he appears in early ballads. Accused of robbing an abbey of money, stock and horses, and killing one of the monks, Godberd ended his days in Newgate Prison. No mention of robbing from the rich and giving to the poor here.

A newly discovered English reference also points to a Robin Hood being active in the reign of Edward I. Written around 1460 in Latin by a monk, it appears in the margin of the *Polychronicon* – a compilation of the knowledge of the age – found in Eton College library. It says:

> Around this time, according to popular opinion, a certain outlaw named Robin Hood, with his accomplices, infested Sherwood and other law-abiding areas of England with continuous robberies.

But in 1521, a third Scotsman named John Major published his *History of Great Britain*, assigning Robin and Little John to the years of Richard I's captivity in Austria, 1193–4. He wrote:

> About this time it was, as I conceive, that there flourished those most famous robbers Robert Hood, an Englishman, and Little John, who lay in wait in the woods, but spoiled of their goods those only that were wealthy. They took the life of no man, unless he either attacked them or offered resistance in defence of his property. Robert supported by his plundering one hundred bowmen, ready fighters every one, with whom four hundred of the strongest would not dare to engage in combat. The feats of this Robert are told in song all over Britain. He would allow no woman to suffer injustice, nor would he spoil the poor, but rather enriched them from the plunder taken from the abbots. The robberies of this man I condemn, but of all robbers he was the humanest and the chief.

For the word 'chief', Major uses the Latin work '*dux*', which can also mean duke, implying for the first time that Robin Hood might have had some aristocratic associations.

Like Wyntoun and Bower, Major gives no source for his information. It did not come from English historians, as no medieval English historian made any attempt to identify or chronicle the doings of Robin Hood. However, of the three, John Major's date is the best. There is evidence that Robin Hood was a legendary criminal by 1262.

In the late thirteenth century the surname Robinhood – and its variants Rabunhod, Robehod, etc. – began to appear. There were at least eight by 1300. Just as a man who fixed horseshoes might take the name Smith, or a roof-mender might be called Thatcher, Tyler or Slater, a thief or outlaw would be given the surname Robinhood or the like. The earliest recorded example of this occurs in 1262. At Easter that year, the king's remembrancer's memoranda roll notes the pardon of a penalty imposed on the prior of Sandleford for seizing without warrant the chattels of William Robehod, a fugitive. The same case occurs on the roll of the circuit judge in Berkshire in 1261, recording the indictment and outlawing of a criminal gang suspected of robberies and the harbouring of thieves. The gang included one William, son of Robert le Fevre, whose chattels had been seized by the prior of Sandleford. There is no doubt that the William Robehod of the memoranda roll and the William, son of Robert le Fevre, of the plea roll were one and the same person. Someone along the administrative channel from the Berkshire circuit to the king's remembrancer changed the name. He probably did so because William, son of Robert, had Robert in his name and was a member of a gang of outlaws. So he became William Robehod. Whoever changed the name knew that Robin Hood was an exemplary outlaw. Consequently, Robin Hood must have been alive and active some time before Wyntoun's 1283–5 and Bower's 1266, leaving Major's 1193–4, during the absence of King Richard and exactly the time recorded in legend.

There is further evidence that a real Robin Hood existed around that time. According to the records of York assizes of 1225, one Robert Hod, a fugitive, failed to appear before the justices and was thus outlawed. At Michaelmas the following year, his chattels – worth 32 shillings and 6 pence in all – were forfeit to the exchequer. There is no record of the charges against him. The account recurs the following year. However, the outlaw's name is then given the more colloquial form 'Hobbehod'. In the margin, there is a note that the amount is due from the Liberty of St Peter's, York – more commonly known as York Minster. In other words, the outlaw had lived in the archbishopric.

John Ball, the English Lollard priest who was prominent in the Peasants Revolt of 1381, told the rebels 'biddeth Piers Plowman go to his work and chastise wel Hobbe the Robbere'. This suggest that Hobbe, possibly a diminutive of Robin or Robinhood, was a sobriquet used colloquially for thieves. The Lollards were followers of the radical theologian John Wycliffe, a pre-Reformation religious dissenter. And the Lollard attitude to the Catholic Church permeates the tale of Robin Hood, who regularly steals from rich priests.

In 1381, a man named Robert Robynhod was living in Winchelsea in Sussex, and a manuscript in Lincoln Cathedral dating from the early fifteenth century mentions 'Robin Hood in Scherewood stod', echoing the 'Robin Hood in Sarnsdale stock' of the 1429 Court of Common Pleas. In an early edition of the collection of religious tracts called *Dives and Pauper*, dating from around 1405–10, there is a mention of those who listen to 'a tale or song of Robin Hood or sum rubaudy' rather than hearing Mass or Matins. Around the same time, the monk and Oxford scholar Hugh Legat preached a sermon where he mentioned many men who spoke of 'Robyn Hood that schotte never in his bowe', which is itself a reference to Chaucer's *Troilus and Criseyde*. The same phrase appears again as a proverb in the poem *Reply of Friar Daw Topias* in around 1419–20 and a ship was named 'Robyn Hude' or 'Robert Hude' in Aberdeen in 1438.

John Leland, antiquary to Henry VIII (1509–47) recorded the association between Robin Hood and Barnsdale in his *Itinerary of Britain*, an account of a journey made around 1540. He also said that Robin died in Kirklees. Richard Grafton, the King's printer to Edward VI (1547–53), claimed to have an 'olde and aunciente pamphlet' recording Robin's life. After summarizing Major's story of Robin's life, he says:

> But in an olde and aunciente Pamphlet I finde this written of the sayd Robert Hood. This man (sayth he) discended of a nobel parentage: or rather beyng of a base stocke and linage, was for his manhoode and chivalry advaunced to the noble dignité of an Erle. Excellyng principally in Archery, or shootyng, his manly courage agreeyng thereunto

It then explained how Robin came to be an outlaw.

> But afterwardes he so prodigally exceeded in charges and expences, that he fell into great debt, by reason wherof, so many actions and sutes were commenced against him, wherunto he aunswered not, that by order of lawe he was outlawed, and then for a lewde shift, as his last refuge, gathered together a companye of Roysters and Cutters, and practised robberyes and spoylyng of the kynges subjects, and occupied and frequentede the Forestes or wilde Countries. The which beyng certefyed to the King, and he beyng greatly offended therewith, caused his proclamation to be made that whosoever would bryng him quicke or dead, the king would geve him a great summe of money, as by the recordes in the Exchequer is to be seene

No one collected the reward.

> But of this promise, no man enjoyed any benefite. For the
> sayd Robert Hood, beyng afterwardes troubled with
> sicknesse, came to a certein Nonry in Yorkshire called
> Bircklies [Kirklees?], where desirying to be let blood, he
> was betrayed and bled to deth. After whose death the
> Prioresse of the same place caused him to be buried by the
> high way side, where he had used to rob and spoyle those
> that passed that way

It goes on to mention, intriguingly, an inscribed grave
slab.

> And upon his grave the sayde Prioresse did lay a very
> fayre stone, wherin the names of Robert Hood, William of
> Goldesborough and others were graven. And the cause
> why she buryed him there was for that the common
> passengers and travailers knowyng and seeyng him there
> buryed, might more safely and without feare take their
> jorneys that way, which they durst not do in the life of the
> sayd outlawes. And at eyther end of the sayde Tombe was
> erected a crosse of stone, which is to be seene there at this
> present.

Grafton also said that they had seen records in the
exchequer recording the confiscation of his lands, placing
Robin in the reign of Richard I. However, neither the
pamphlet nor the records he refers to have ever been
found. Nevertheless, his rival, the Tudor historian John
Stowe, also repeats Major's assertion that Robin was
active during Richard's imprisonment.

In the Sloane collection in the British Library, there is

a short prose *Life of Robin Hood*. Though it purports to be factual, it is probably based on earlier ballads. It gives Robin's birthplace as Locksley. There is a Loxley in Warwickshire, but it is thought that the manuscript is referring to Loxley outside Sheffield in Yorkshire.

There is more, rather confusing evidence about Robin's death in Kirklees. In *The True Tale of Robin Hood* published in 1632, the author Martin Parker said that Robin died on 4 December 1198 and recorded his epitaph which read:

> Robert Earle of Huntington
> Lies under this little stone.
> No archer was like him so good:
> His wildnesse named him Robin Hood.
> Full thirteene years, and something more
> These northerne parts he vexes sore.
> Such out-lawes as he and his men
> May England never know again.

This has largely been discounted because, until the sixteenth century, Robin was a lowly yeoman – a smallholder. Leland called him 'nobilis' – which means noble in either moral or class terms, possibly both. He only became an earl with Grafton in 1562, becoming the earl of Huntington in two plays by Anthony Munday in 1598. In 1746, the Lincolnshire antiquary and natural philosopher, Dr William Stukeley even gave the earl of Huntington a spurious pedigree.

However, when the Dean of York, Thomas Gale, died in 1702, he left among his papers a similar epitaph said to have been written on Robin's grave. It read:

Hear undernead this laitl stean
Lais Robert earl of Huntington
Nea arcir ver as hei sae geud
An pipl kauld im robin heud
Sick utlaws as hi an is men
Vil England never si agen.

(Here underneath this little stone
Lies Robert earl of Huntington
No archer was as he so good
And people called him Robin Hood
Such outlaws as he and his men
Will England never see again.)

Gale gives the date of Robin's death, as carved into the gravestone, as 'Obiit 24 kal dekembris 1247' – the 24 *kalends* December 1247. The *kalends* is the first day of the month in the Roman calendar, the day money is due. Indeed, the *kalends* is what gives us the word calendar. The Romans dated their days back from the *kalends*, so 24 *kalends* December would be equivalent to 7 November. However, *kalends* coincided with the New Moon and the Romans also used the *nones*, or half moons, and ides, or full moons, in their calculations. So 7 November would have been the *nones* and the construction 24 *kalends* December would not have been used, which, as a scholar, Thomas Gale would have known. It is thought to be a jocular reference to Christmas – the date you could arrive at if you counted 24 days forward from the *kalends*.

However, at Kirklees there was unquestionably a grave slab. Richard Grafton referred to it in his *Chronicle*. The Elizabethan historian and traveller William Camden mentioned it in the fifth edition of his *Britannia* published in 1607. Then antiquary and political pamphleteer Nathaniel Johnston, who practiced medicine in Pontefract less than twenty miles from Kirklees, made a drawing of it that appeared in Richard Gough's *Sepulchral Monuments of Great Britain* of 1789. By Gough's day, though, the slab was much 'broken and defaced'. Bits of it had been chiselled away by local people who believed it had curative powers. Notwithstanding the damage, the first part of an inscription could be made out. It was said to have read: 'Here lies Robin Hude, William Goldburgh, Thomas –'. Grafton had mentioned the name William of Goldesborough on the grave slab two hundred years before. There is no mention of William Goldburgh or William of Goldesborough or Thomas in the legend of Robin Hood and the grave was more than bow-and-arrow range of the gatehouse of the old Priory, given the type of bow he had available and the fact that Robin would have been old and decrepit at the time. However, Gough believes that the stone had been moved. A new inscription based on the Gale epitaph was added in the nineteenth century.

The eighteenth-century antiquary Joseph Ritson compiled a book, *Robin Hood: a collection of all the ancient poems, songs, and ballads now extant related to that celebrated English outlaw*, which was published in 1795. He said in his introduction 'The Life of Robin Hood' that Robin died 'on the 18th of November, 1247, being the 31st year of king Henry II, and (if the date assigned to his birth be correct) about the 87th of his age'. He does not say how he knows this, but the year and month of his death agrees with the date from the inscription on Robin's grave slab found in Thomas Gale's papers.

Despite all the caveats, a shadowy biography of Robin Hood emerges. He was born in Loxley around 1160 and was an active outlaw around 1193–4, then outlawed again in 1225 until his death in 1247. This coincides with the twenty-two years that *A Lytell Geste of Robyn Hode*, one of the earliest ballads, says that Robin was an outlaw and points to the Yorkshire outlaw Robin Hod, who already had his gangster name 'Hobbehod' by 1226. By 1262, his name was legend and there were more 'Robinhoods' whose criminal activities only added to his status. In 1605, Guy Fawkes and his co-conspirators were referred to as 'Robin Hoods' by Robert Cecil, secretary of state to Elizabeth I and James I of England.

The seventeenth-century antiquary Roger Dodsworth came up with another story. He writes of a 'Robert Locksley, born in Bradfield parish, in Hallamshire [south Yorkshire]. . . [who] wounded his stepfather with a plough: fled into the woods, and was relieved by his mother till he was discovered'. He then went to 'Clifton upon Calder, and came acquainted with Little John, that kept kine [cows]; which said John is buried at Hathershead [Hathersage] in Derbyshire, where he hath a fair tomb-stone with an inscription'. Dodsworth then throws in the idea that it may be Little John, the cowman, rather than Robert Locksley, the ploughman, who was the nobleman, though he distances himself from it, saying 'Mr Long saith that Fabyan saith, Little John was an earl of Huntingdon'. It was Huntingdon here, rather than Huntington. Both spellings were used for Huntington, though not for Huntingdon, Cambridgeshire.

Nevertheless, the idea persisted that Robin Hood was of noble birth. Stukeley's pedigree drawn up in 1746 traces Robin's line back to a marriage between Gilbert de

Gaunt and 'Roisia', daughter of Richard Fitzgilbert. Both de Gaunt and Fitzgilbert were lords of the Norman settlement, following the conquest. Unfortunately, Fitzgilbert's daughter Rohaise de Clare died before de Gaunt was born. Despite this, Stukeley, gives them a daughter named Maud, who married Ralf Fitzooth, another Norman who, according to Stukeley, was lord of Kyme. The pedigree of the lords of Kyme in Lincolnshire is well established and leaves no room for Ralf Fitzooth. Nevertheless, Stukely says their son William Fitzooth was brought up by Robert, earl of Oxford, and married the daughter of Payn Beauchamp and Lady Roisia de Vere. This union was then said to have produced 'Robert Fitzooth, commonly called Robin Hood, pretended earl of Huntington'. This name 'Fitzooth' or 'fitz Ooth' is otherwise unknown, though there was a William fitz Otuel or fitz Othuel who lived in the middle of the twelfth century and who had claims on the lands of his maternal grandfather, Eudo Dapifer, the real husband of Rohaise.

Bishop Thomas Percy, author of *Reliques of Ancient English Poetry* published in 1765, pours more cold water on this pedigree. According to Percy

the most ancient poems on Robin Hood make no mention of his earldom. He is expressly asserted to have been a yeoman in a very old legend in verse preserved in the archives of the public library at Cambridge in eight fyttes, or parts, printed in black letter, quarto thus inscribed: 'Here begynneth a lytell geste of Robyn Hode and his meyne, and of the proude sheryfe of Notyngham'.

To rub in his point, he quotes the first verse:

> Lithe and lysten, gentylmen
> That be for fre-bore blode:
> I shall you tell of a good yeman,
> His name was Robyn hode
>
> (Harken and listen, gentlemen
> That be of freeborn blood
> I shall tell you of a good yeoman,
> His name was Robin Hood.)

In his 'The Life of Robin Hood', Joseph Ritson acknowledges Bishop Percy's criticism, but still maintains that Robin Hood was 'frequently styled, and commonly reputed to have been the earl of Huntingdon; a title to which, in the latter part of his life, at least, he actually appears to have had some sort of pretension'. He also notes that Stukeley's pedigree was unsupported by the facts, but reproduces Robert Fitzooth's family tree. So Ritson's account inextricably mixes fact and fiction.

The nineteenth-century historian and Unitarian minister Joseph Hunter wrote several volumes about South Yorkshire before moving to London in 1833 to become assistant keeper of public records at the new Public Record Office. Part of his job was to edit and publish the records of the medieval governments in England. In that capacity, he began his search for the real Robin Hood – the man behind the figure in the early ballads.

A Lytell Geste of Robyn Hode, the ballad that Bishop Percy quoted from, mentions 'Edwarde, our comly kynge' who came to Nottingham to arrest Robin Hood for taking his deer. However, after feasting with Robin in disguise in the forest, the King reveals himself and takes Robin with him to court. But Robin longed for the forest and returned home.

Hunter noted that this could have occurred on only one known royal progress, which proceeded through Lancashire and Yorkshire, and then to Nottingham, from April to November 1323. He also discovered that, between 24 March and 22 November 1324, a Robyn Hode was employed in royal service as a *valet de chambre*, but left the king's service 'because he could no longer work'. Then Hunter found a Robert Hood and his wife Matilda in the court rolls of the manor of Wakefield, just ten miles from Barnsdale, in the years 1316 and 1317. Other records show that a man named Robert Hood was in the area at the time. He was mustered to fight the Scots in 1318 and fined thruppence for failing to answer the call, though his name does not appear in subsequent musters.

Hunter went on to argue that the Robert Hood of Wakefield had become an outlaw after joining the rebellion of Thomas, earl of Lancaster, which ended with Lancaster's defeat by Edward II at the battle of Boroughbridge in 1322. After Lancaster was executed at Pontefract, Hunter says that Robert Hood made his peace with the king and went into his service, only to return to his old haunts a year later. Matilda, Hunter suggests, was the original Maid Marian. He also put forward a candidate for the double-crossing prioress of Kirklees – Elizabeth Staynton, a daughter of the minor gentry, who Hunter discovered might that been related to Hood. However, Hunter does not prove that the Robyn Hode in royal service and the Robert Hood of Wakefield are the same man – by that time the names Robyn and Robert, Hode and Hood were commonplace. Nor is there any evidence of either of them being outlawed. Indeed his name is not among the 'Contrariants' – followers of the earl of Lancaster – in Wakefield who were dispossessed after the failure of the Lancastrian rebellion.

What's more, a fragment of the day-book of the royal chamber for the period 14 April to 7 July 1323 has survived. Read under ultraviolet light, it reveals that the *valet de chambre* Robyn Hode was paid his wage on 27 June 1323, over four months before the King visited Nottingham from 9 to 23 November that year. Although this effectively sinks Hunter's theory, his research did show that the Hoods were well established in the Barnsdale area and that one of them – a Robert Hood the Grave who was penalized for breaking the lord of the manor's fold at Alverthorpe – was a criminal. But this is not our man. Barnsdale was already known as an area inhabited by outlaws and there were Robin Hoods all over the country by then. In 1296, a Gilbert Robynhod appears in Fletching, East Sussex, and, in 1325, a Katherine Robynhod appears in the London coroner's roll.

There are other Robert or Robin Hoods that might have contributed to the legend. Robert Hood, servant of Alexander Nequam, abbot of Circencester, killed Ralph of Circencester in the abbot's garden some time between 1213 and 1216. Another Robin Hood languished in prison in 1354, awaiting trial for offences committed in the forest of Rockingham. While Circencester in Gloucestershire is a bit out of the way, Rockingham Forest abuts Sherwood. However, the Robin Hood imprisoned there was hardly the successful outlaw of legend.

The nineteenth-century antiquarian J.R. Planche further muddied the waters. In 1864, he published a paper called

'A Ramble with Robin Hood' in the Report of the Association of Architects where he took a fresh look at Stukeley's genealogy of the Fitzooth family. In the twelfth century, spelling had not been fixed and names often appeared in a number of forms. Even as late as the sixteenth century it is possible to find Shakespeare's name spelt in numerous different ways – Shaksper, Shaxpere, Shagsphere. So Fitzooth might appear as fitz Ooth or Fitz Othe. In Middle English, the 'th' sound was often represented by a double D – as in modern Welsh where Gwynedd is pronounced Gwyneth. Sometimes a double D becomes a single D and Planche maintained that the name Fitz Othe could easily have been written as Fitz Ode, which is a short step from Fitz Odo.

Planche had discovered that the Fitz Odo family lived in Loxley, Warwickshire, during the reign of Richard I. He believed that Robin Hood was Robert Fitz Odo, the lord of Loxley Manor from the reign of Henry II until 1196. He appears in Dugdale's *Baronage* of 1675 and the records of the nearby priory of Kenilworth show that they bought land from him in the late twelfth century.

The prefix Fitz means 'the illegitimate son of'. Norman nobles often used it to show they descended from some famous or landed person. In this case, Robert Fitz Odo could be descended from William the Conqueror's half brother Odo, bishop of Bayeux. Despite being a bishop, Odo had a number of illegitimate sons. Sometimes to remove the taint of illegitimacy, the Fitz was dropped, so Robert Odo, or Robert Ode, could easily have been Robin Hode, as Robin Hood's name often appears.

There are some curious things about the life of Robert Odo. According to the *Curia Register* (Register of Arms) he was no longer a knight in 1196, though commercial records show that he was alive and living in Harbury, just eight miles from Loxley, in 1203. Caught up in the rivalry between Richard I and his brother John, he seems to have been disinherited by Richard, then reinstated when John came to the throne in 1199, though he did not move back into Loxley Manor, which was occupied by his daughter Basilia. At the very least, tales from Robert Fitz Odo's life could have fed through into the *Lytell Geste of Robin Hood* and the fourteenth-century romance *Fouke le Fitz Waryn*.

There is another link between Robert Odo, Loxley in Warwickshire and Robin Hood. In the graveyard at Loxley is a grave slab that is strikingly similar to the one drawn by Nathaniel Johnson in 1665. It bears an inscription to 'Constance', a member of the Cove Jones family who owned Loxley Hall in the nineteenth century. But the stone itself is much older.

By the fifteenth century, the name of Robin Hood was mixed up in political insurrection as well as criminal activity. In 1439 a parliamentary petition from Tutbury in Staffordshire complained that a gentleman from Aston named Piers Venables rescued a prisoner on the first Sunday after Christmas and escaped into the forest. He then

> gadered and assembled unto hym many misdoers . . . and, in manere of insurrection, wente into the wodes in that contre, like as it hadde been Robyn Hobe and his meyne

His band were described as 'yomen' and they 'kepyn the wodes and strang contrays' and seem to have supported themselves by robbing. In 1441, a group of yeomen and labours blocked the road in Southacre, Norfolk, singing

'We are Robynhodesmen war war war' and threatened to kill a certain Sir Geoffrey Harsyk. The matter came before the King's Bench. In 1450, one Jack Cade took 'Robin Hood' as his *nom de guerre* in a rising against the enclosures, where landowners started fencing off common land. Sir John Conyers called himself Robin of Redesdale – or Robin Mend-all – when he took up arms against the Yorkist government in 1496. His equivalent in Yorkshire, Robin of Holderness, was probably Robert Hillyard of Winestead. Then, in 1498, Roger Marshall of Wednesbury, Staffordshire, used the alias Robin Hood when he led a gang of a hundred men in an affray at Willenhall. The civic authorities in Walsall feared that Marshall and his followers were aiming to free two men from prison and had banned them from the fair at Willenhall that was to be held that Trinity Sunday, a week after Whitsun. The matter was brought before the court of the Star Chamber. But Marshall defended himself that he had dressed as Robin Hood – with one of his captains as the Abbot of Marham, one of the local lords of misrule – to gather money for the church and denied that he had any intent of causing a riot.

Although many of the themes and details of the tales of Robin Hood and his Merry Men have been borrowed from elsewhere, it seems clear that there was a seed of truth around which they coalesced. However, reviewing the earliest references to the great hero of Merry Olde England, it also seems clear that he was nothing like the loveable rogue portrayed by Howard Pyle and movies and TV series throughout the twentieth century.

3

THE HERO OF THE BALLADS

The oldest known ballad about Robin Hood is called 'Robin Hood and the Monk'. It has existed in manuscript form from about 1450 and was found among a collection of manuscripts that included a prayer pleading for protection against thieves and robbers. However, it was thought to have been recited, rather than sung as it ends with the lines:

> Thus endys the talkyng of the munke
> And Robyn Hode i-wysse;
> God, that is euer a crowned kyng,
> Bryng vs all to his blisse.

(Thus ends the talking of the monk
And Robyn Hode certainly;
God, that is ever a crowned king,
Bring us all to his bliss.)

The poem begins with a paean on the greenwood on a May morning, but Robin is unhappy because he has not been to church for a fortnight and decides to go to pray to the Virgin at St Mary's in Nottingham. 'Moche the mylner sun' – usually rendered as Much the miller's son, though Pyle calls him Midge – advises Robin to take twelve men with him, but Robin insists he only needs Little John. On the way, they make a bet on their skill as archers. Little John wins, but Robin welches on the bet. They quarrel. Robin hits Little John who, after threatening Robin with his sword, leaves in a huff.

Arriving at the church alone, Robin is recognized by a grey-haired monk, who calls the Sheriff. In the ensuing fight, Robin kills twelve of the Sheriff's men. But when he strikes the Sheriff on the head, his sword breaks in two, leaving him defenceless. The manuscript is incomplete and the next part of the poem is missing. The tale resumes with the outlaws' shock at the news that Robin has been captured. Little John and Much set out to rescue Robin. On the way, they meet the monk. They win his confidence by pretending to be victims of Robin Hood. Then they kill the perfidious monk, along with his page.

Little John and Much then take the monk's letter of accreditation to the King, telling him that the monk died on the way. He makes them yeomen of the crown and gives them the royal seal as authorization to get Robin and bring him to him. Returning to Nottingham, Little John and Much dine with the Sheriff. When he falls into a drunken sleep, they visit the jail, gaining entry by telling the jailer that Robin has escaped. They then kill the jailer, free Robin, leap from the castle walls and return to Sherwood.

As Little John has repaid Robin's bad turn with a good one, Robin offers John command of the outlaw band, but John says he would prefer to follow Robin. The Sheriff is afraid that he will be hanged for dereliction of duty, but the King tells him they have both been fooled.

In the poem there is a mention of 'oure cumly kyng', which is usually taken as a reference to the notably handsome Edward IV (1461–70, 1471–83). This would date the poem to later than 1461. However, the same phrase was sometimes used to describe Edward III (1327–77). This could make it the oldest of the existing 'rhymes of Robin Hood' referred to by Langland in *Piers Plowman*.

There are notable parallels between this ballad and the extended *Adam Bell, Clym of the Cloughe and Wyllyam of Cloudeslee*, which was in print in 1557, but seems to have originated much earlier. Like Robin, the three men in the title were 'outlawed for venison', live in the greenwood and outwit the sheriff and even the King by guile. But they were based not in Barnsdale, Sherwood or Nottingham, but in Inglewood near Carlisle in Cumbria.

William of Cloudesley goes into Carlisle because he misses his wife and child, but is betrayed by an old woman he had befriended out of charity. After a fight, William is seized. While a gallows is being erected, a small boy goes to tell Adam and Clim what has happened. They gain entry into Carlisle by persuading the porter they are carrying the King's writ and seal. Then they kill him.

In the town square Adam and Clim shoot down the sheriff and the justice with their bows and arrows, and release their friend. They escape back to the forest leaving many dead. Adam, Clim and William head for London where they ask for a pardon for killing the King's deer. The King is not amenable, but is persuaded by the queen. Then the news arrives of what they have done in Carlisle. But the King has already promised them a pardon.

There is an archery contest with William of Cloudesley showing his skill by splitting a hazel wand at 400 paces. He also shoots an apple off his son's head, which is reminiscent of William Tell. Adam, Clim and William then give up being outlaws and become yeomen of the queen's chamber. William's wife becomes chief gentle-woman and governess of the nursery.

Adam Bell, Clim of the Clough and William of Cloudesley got mixed up with Robin Hood and his Merry Men early on. The first reference to Bell and his gang appears in the 1432 Parliament Roll for Wiltshire. Added to a list of local members, presumably in a spirit of satire, are a sequence of outlaw names. It begins 'Adam Belle, Clym O'Cluw, Willyam Cloudesle', then continues 'Robyn Hode . . . Lytel Joon, Muchette Millerson, Scathelok, Reynoldyn'.

Around 1475, *A Gest of Robyn Hode*, also known as *A Lyttel Geste of Robin Hode*, appeared. Gest or geste can means exploits, or a tale told in verse. Probably compiled from earlier stories, it has 456 four-line stanzas, divided into eight 'fyttes' or cantos. The *Gest* proved popular with early printers. No fewer than five editions were produced between the last years of the fifteenth century and the middle of the sixteenth century. Essentially a minstrel's serial, it was designed to be recited in instalments – sixteenth-century soap opera.

It begins with a familiar tale. Robin refuses to eat until

he has a guest for dinner. Little John, Much the miller's son, and Will Scarlok (Scarlet) go out to find one. They come across a poorly dressed knight. He accepts the invitation to dinner. At the end of the meal Robin suggests that he pays for it, but the knight says he has a mere ten shillings on his person. When Little John has verified this, Robin asks how a knight of the realm has become so impoverished.

The knight explains that his son has killed a man and, to raise the bail, he has spent all his money and mortgaged his land to the abbot of St Mary's, York, for £400. Robin decides to lend the knight the money, pledged on the name of the Virgin Mother, and Little John, Much the miller's son and Scarlok insist on giving him new clothes and a suitable horse. When the knight leaves, Little John accompanies him as his attendant.

The knight, still in his rags, turns up on the last day the mortgage can be paid and needles the abbot about his lack of charity. Eventually, he produces the £400 and redeems his lands, much to the abbot's annoyance. The knight then saves up the money to repay Robin, and also buys a hundred bows and arrows fletched with peacock feathers to give him as a reward. But, on his way to repay the debt, he is delayed by a wrestling match, where he had to save one contestant – a stranger – from the mob.

Meanwhile, Little John has won an archery contest and has been taken into the service of the Sheriff. But one day he wakes late and wants to eat, precipitating a fight with the steward, the bottler and the cook because it is not meal time. When the cook proves a tough adversary, Little John proposes that he comes to the greenwood and joins the outlaws. The cook agrees and feeds Little John, then they plunder the Sheriff's silver. Back in the forest, Robin is suspicious, but the cook says that the Sheriff has sent the silver as a present. Little John then tricks the Sheriff into coming into the forest, saying there are green deer there, then introduces Robin as the 'master hart'. The Sheriff complains that Little John has betrayed him, but John says it is the Sheriff's own fault as he has not been well provided for in his home. The Sheriff is forced to eat off the silverware Little John and the cook have stolen from his and sleep under the greenwood tree. One night in the forest is enough for him. In the morning, he is permitted to go – but only after he has sworn that, in future, he would do no harm to Robin and his men.

Once again Robin sends out Little John, Much the miller's son and Will Scarlok to find him a guest for dinner. This time they find a monk from St Mary's, but he will only accompany them after they have seen off his escort. After the feast, the monk claims to have only 20 marks. In his travelling chest they find £800. Robin takes it, claiming that St Mary, the Virgin Mother, has sent it to him, repaying him two-fold for his generosity to the sorrowful knight.

The knight then arrives. He explains that he is late because he had to save a yeoman at the wrestling. Robin tells him that whoever helps a fellow yeoman is his friend, and refuses to accept the £400 repayment. When the knight gives him his gift of the bows and arrows, Robin gives him half the £800 he has taken from the monk.

The Sheriff holds an archery contest. The prize is an arrow made of gold and silver. Robin and his men take part and Robin, inevitably, wins. Even though he has given his word not to, the Sheriff tries to seize Robin. In the melee, Little John is wounded in the knee. Robin and the Merry Men escape and find refuge in the castle of

Sir Richard at the Lee – although he is first named at this point, it is plain that this is the same knight that appeared earlier in the ballad. The gates are shut and they feast in safety.

The Sheriff then besieges the castle. After a confrontation, Sir Richard heads off to take the advice of the King, who insists he must detain Robin. Meanwhile, Robin and his men have returned to the forest. The Sheriff takes his revenge by waylaying Sir Richard and taking him prisoner. Sir Richard's wife then turns to Robin for help. Robin kills the Sheriff, felling him with an arrow then hacking his head off with a sword. The Merry Men see off the sheriff's men and release Sir Richard, who accompanies them to the greenwood until he can arrange a pardon for Robin and his men from the King.

Meanwhile, the King has come to Nottingham to strip Sir Richard of his lands, offering them to anyone who will kill Sir Richard. But no one is interested in taking them over with Robin Hood still at large. The King is further outraged to see that Robin and the outlaws have been slaughtering his deer.

At length, the King is persuaded to use guile to ensnare Robin. He disguises himself as an abbot and his men as monks, and they head out into the forest. Robin and his men waylay them and take half the £40 they are carrying. After the obligatory feast, the outlaws hold an archery contest. The penalty for missing the target is a clout on the head. Robin hands out the punishment with gusto, but when he himself misses the mark, the abbot steps forward to administer the blow. He knocks Robin to the ground, then reveals himself to be the King. Robin, his men and Sir Richard all fall to their knees. They are pardoned and enter royal service.

The King takes Robin to court, but Robin longs for his old life in the forest. He obtains permission to visit a chapel he has founded in Barnsdale. Out in the greenwood he cannot resist shooting one of the King's deer. Then he blows on his horn to recall his old band of outlaws. Together they live in the forest for the next twenty-two years – perhaps the same twenty-two years between 1225, when the fugitive Robin Hod was declared an outlaw at York assizes, and 1247 when Robin Hood was thought to have died.

Needing medical treatment Robin visits the Prioress of Kirklees, 'that near was of his kin'. But she has a secret lover, Roger of Doncaster, and the two of them plot the outlaw's death. They decided to do this by having the Prioress bleed Robin – medical bloodletting was a common practice until the late nineteenth century. Robin dies and the poem ends with the poet asking for Christ to have mercy on his soul.

> For he was a good outlawe,
> And dyde pore men moch god.

Interestingly, the action in *A Gest of Robyn Hode* moves back and forth between Barnsdale, Sherwood and Nottingham. This may indicate that the *Gest* was compiled from earlier works, embracing the two main geographical traditions. But by 1475, many of the major elements of the Robin Hood tale we know today were already in place.

Robin's demise is related separately in *The Death of Robin Hood*. A damaged copy from the mid-seventeenth century exists, but the poem seems have been written much earlier. In it, Robin is on his way to 'Churchlees' (Kirklees) to have his blood let by his cousin, the Prioress.

Will Scarlet urges him to take a bodyguard of a hundred bowmen, but Robin insists that he need take only Little John. However, when the bleeding is taking place, Robin realizes his cousin's treachery. He blows his horn to summon Little John. The two of them are trying to escape when Robin is stabbed in the side by 'Red Roger' – who is presumably the same man as Roger of Doncaster in the *Gest*. Robin kills Red Roger, but is mortally wounded. Little John wants to burn down the hall, Kirklees, in revenge, but Robin stops him.

> 'If I shold doe any widow hurt, at my latter end,
> God,' he said, 'wold blame me.
>
> 'I never hurt fair maid in all my time,
> Nor at mine end shall it be,
> But give me my bent bow in my hand,
> And a broad arrow I'll let flee;
> And where this arrow is taken up,
> There shall my grave digged be.'

There he wanted to be buried under the green sod with his bow at his side.

Another early ballad, *Robin Hood and the Potter*, exists in manuscript form from the late fifteenth or, more probably, early sixteenth century. It introduces the idea of Robin disguising himself as a potter, an idea probably borrowed from Hereward the Wake, the Saxon freedom fighter. The ballad begins with Little John warning Robin about the potter – a tough customer as Little John has already learnt to his cost. Robin ignores this advice and is determined to charge the potter a toll to travel through the forest. He waylays the potter and they fight. Although the potter is only armed with a staff, against Robin's sword and buckler – a small shield held in the hand – the potter wins easily and tells Robin that it is very discourteous to hinder poor yeomen when they are going about their business.

Robin then befriends the potter and persuades him to change clothes so Robin can go into Nottingham in disguise. The potter agrees, provided Robin sells his pots. But Robin under-prices the pots. Soon there are only five left which he gives to the Sheriff's wife. In exchange, he receives an invitation to dinner. After dinner there is an archery contest. Robin can scarcely conceal his mastery of the bow and arrow and, in conversation, admits that he knows Robin Hood. They had shot together a hundred times under his 'trysting tree' and promises to take the Sheriff there the following day.

When they reach the forest, Robin blows on his horn and the outlaws appear. They take the Sheriff's horse, but Robin stops anything worse happening to him because the Sheriff's wife has been so kind to him. The Sheriff is allowed to return home to his wife on foot and Robin pays the potter £10 for his wares.

There are a number of elements missing from these early ballads. There is no Maid Marian. Instead Robin is devoted to the Virgin Mary. And there is no Friar Tuck. The monks and friars that appear are usually a bad lot. Although bows and arrows are used, Robin and his men do most of their fighting with swords. The staff as a weapon appears only in the hands of the potter. Little John is a friend from the beginning, along with Much the miller's son and Will Scarlet.

The only King mentioned is Edward. Richard or John are nowhere to be seen. There is no indication that Robin or his men have become outlaws because of oppressive taxes. The only tax mentioned is in the 'pavage' or toll that Robin seeks to extract from the potter – and that is only one penny. Indeed the only financial oppression suffered is by the knight at the hands of the monk.

There is no indication that Robin is part of any Saxon resistance movement fighting back against the Normans – indeed, in the *Gest*, he is reconciled with the King. He is not a rebel who advocates the killing of landowners. Nor is he part of an agrarian revolt against rents, manorial services and the social hierarchy of the kind that resulted in the Peasant's Revolt of 1381. That was centred on Kent and East Anglia, while Robin was from Nottinghamshire or south Yorkshire. Nor was he a peasant, any more than he was a knight or a dispossessed nobleman. He was empathetically a yeoman.

Complaints about taxes and bailiffs appear in other ballads of the time, but the tales of Robin Hood make no mention of robbing the rich to give to the poor. In the *Gest*, Robin tells Little John to do no harm to husbandmen, yeomen, 'nor any knight nor any squire who will be a good fellow'. The sorrowful knight is a 'good fellow' who should be helped. The only enemies identified are clerics and the Sheriff of Nottingham. The King goes in and out of favour. And then there is Red Roger.

4

THE LITERARY TRADITION

In medieval Europe, May Day was an important festival. It probably had its origins in ancient agricultural rituals to ensure the fertility of crops and, by extension, livestock and human beings. The Greeks and Romans held such festivals. In England, people gathered wild flowers and green branches. They decorated a May tree and danced around it, and they crowned a king and queen of the May.

Such practices were considered licentious and pagan by the Puritans, who tried to stamp them out. Consequently the tradition was never transplanted to the United States. But in fifteenth- and sixteenth-century England the May festivities were still going strong. By then, pageants were held to raise money for the community. They were often headed by a man playing Robin Hood, who would carry a bow and arrow and be surrounded by forest imagery. Funds raised this way were used to buy a new silver censer in Henley on Thames in 1499 and to attend to the roads in Melton in 1556.

Plays were also put on featuring Robin Hood and other figures from the pageant. Nothing survives of the earliest amateur productions. However, the first record of a Robin Hood play is from Exeter in 1426–7. There are mentions of other Robin Hood plays taking place in Wiltshire in 1432, Aberdeen in 1438 and Norfolk in 1441. A fragment of a short play written in the late fifteenth century still exists. It consists of twenty-one couplets written by hand on the upper half of a sheet of paper measuring approximately 8 inches by 10 inches. This is preserved in the library of Trinity College, Cambridge. There is glue on the paper, indicating that, at one time, it was pasted into a larger volume. On the back are some account entries of sums received by one John Stendalle in the fifteenth year of the reign of Edward IV – that is, 1475/6. The handwriting on both sides of the paper are of much the same period, so it is safe to assume that the fragment of the play also originated around 1475 or earlier.

Scholars have linked this manuscript to the household of the well-to-do Norwich gentleman Sir John Paston. In a letter dated April 1473, Paston complained that his horse-keeper had left him and mentions that he had kept him for three years 'to pleye Seynt Jorge and Robyn Hod and the Shryff of Notyngham'. (Saint George was another figure who frequently appeared in the May Games.)

The play is variously known as *Robin Hood and the Sheriff* or *Robin Hood and Guy of Gisborne*. Although the villain is not named in the fragment, some of the action mirrors that in the ballad *Robin Hood and Guy of Gisborne*. It begins with a knight – presumably Sir Guy – and the Sheriff fixing a reward for the capture of Robin Hood. The knight later meets Robin and challenges him to an archery competition. They shoot at a target. Robin cleaves the stick and wins. They then have a stone-throwing contest. Robin wins again. Next they toss a cart axle. Then they wrestle. Robin throws the knight, then the knight throws Robin. Robin blows his horn to summon help, then challenges the knight to a sword-fight to the death. Robin cuts off the knight's head and dresses in his clothes, hiding the severed head in the hood of his cloak.

In a second scene, two outlaws – possibly Little John and Will Scarlet – meet. One tells the other that Robin has been captured by the Sheriff. They agree to set out on foot to kill the Sheriff. On the way, they meet Friar Tuck, bow in hand, who is single-handedly holding off the Sheriff and his men. They are surrounded, captured and bound. They are taken to the gates of the prison. The Sheriff calls for Robin to be brought out and hanged. The gates are opened. It is assumed that some sort of scuffle ensues (this is not written down) but the Sheriff and his men are overcome and Robin and his men escape.

With only the dialogue remaining (there are no stage directions or indication of who is speaking) it is difficult to make out precisely what is going on. However, it is clear that there was plenty of action. Such a play would have been staged outdoors, perhaps in a field, so the archery competition, stone throwing, axle tossing, wrestling match and a sword fight would provide plenty of entertainment.

By the end of the fifteenth century the figure of Robin
Hood was widely known through the games. Many
towns and villages had replaced their traditional king of
the May – also known as the Summer Lord, the Lord of
Misrule or the Abbot of Bon Accord – with Robin Hood
attended by Little John, Friar Tuck and Merry Men
playing pipes. Robin appeared at the May fair in
Crosscombe in Somerset in 1476. He was plainly a
familiar figure at the Willenhall fair in 1498, where Roger
Marshall was charged with affray. Robin Hood also
appeared at the games in Wells in 1498, at Reading in
1498–9 and at Kingston-upon-Thames in 1507. In
Scotland, he had arrived in Edinburgh by 1492 and in
Aberdeen in 1508. There, in an order dated 17 November
1508, it was announced that the traditional procession
through the town would be led by 'Robert huyd and litile
John' formally known as the 'Abbot and priour of
Bonacord'. A certain amount of dressing up was required.
The churchwarden's accounts of Kingston-upon-Thames
for the years 1507–29 show regular expenditure for the
banner, coat, gloves and shoes of 'Robyn Hode'. In
records kept in Yeovil, it was clear that men waited years
to play Robin Hood – and those that did had almost
always served as churchwardens. However, from 1578 on,
Robin Hood was replaced as leader of the Whitsun
festivities in Yeovil by the 'keeper of the ale'.

During the sixteenth century Robin remained one of
the most widely represented figures in the springtime
festival, though other traditional figures did carry on. One
of Bishop Hugh Latimers sermons in 1549 referred to a
visit he had made to a town some years before –
apparently in the 1530s – where the church was empty on
a Sunday because, he was told, 'it is Robin Hoodes day.

The parishe are gone abroad to gather for Robyn Hoote.'
In May 1607, the 'Lord of the May' procession at Wells
included Robin Hood and his men as one of ten groups of
traditional characters.

Alongside the Lord of Misrule, Robin Hood
represented anarchy. He was a rebel against the normal
order of things, rather than the righter of wrongs he
became later. However, he was carrying some historical
baggage. In his battles with the Sheriff of Nottingham, he
was openly defiant of constituted authority – even the
King. Sir Richard Morison complained to Henry VIII
of the

> plays of Robin Hood, Maid Marian, Friar Tuck, wherein
> besides the lewdness and ribawdry that there is opened to
> the people, disobedience also to your officers is taught,
> whilst these good bloods go about to take from the Sheriff
> of Nottingham one that for offending the laws should
> have suffered execution.

He said they should be forbidden, while other plays
should be devised showing the 'abomination and wickedness of the bishop of Rome, monks, friars, nuns and such
like'.

Some academics have maintained that the portrayal of
the anti-authoritarian Robin acted as a safety valve against
social unrest. At least one contemporary said that all the
mock fighting involved was a useful preparation for war in
times when England faced invasion. This was at a time
when every Englishman between 17 and 60 who was not
lame, decrepit or maimed, a priest, a justice or a 'baron of
the exchequer' was required to keep a longbow and arrows
in his house and practise shooting on a Sunday afternoon.

Any man who had a 'man-child' between 7 and 17 in his house had to keep a bow and two shafts to teach the boy archery. If the boy was a servant, the price of the bow and arrows could be deducted from his wages. Once the boy reached 17, he had to provide the bow and arrows himself.

Despite Henry VIII's general disapproval of Robin Hood, the outlaw did play a prominent part in the King's own May festivities. According to the *Chronicles* of Edward Hall, first published in 1542, eleven nobles dressed for the May broke into the queen's chamber in 1510:

His grace, therles of Essex, Wilshire, and other noble menne, to the nombre of twelve, cam soudainly in a morning, into the Queen's Chambre, al appareled in shorte cotes, of Kentish Kendal, with hodes on their heddes and hosen of the same, every one of them, his bowes and arrows, and a sword and bucklar, like outlaws, or Rodin Hoode's men, wherefor the Quene, the Ladies, and al other there, were abashed as well for the straunge sight, and also for their soudain comyng, and after certain daunces and pastime made, thei departed.

Then in 1515 Robin Hood played host to the King. Hall wrote of that year's Maying:

The King and Queen accompanied by many lords and ladies rode to the high ground of Shooters Hill to take the open air; and as they passed by the way, they espied a company of tall yeomen, clothed all in green with green hoods and bows and arrows, to the number of two hundred. Then one of them, who called himself Robyn hood, came to the King, desiring him to see his men shoot, and the King was content. Then he whistled, and all the two hundred archers shot and loosed at once, and then he whistled again, and they likewise shot again; their arrows whistled by craft of the head, so that the noise was strange and great, and much pleased the King and Queen and all the company. All these archers were of the King's guard and apparelled themselves to make solace to the King. The Robyn desired the King and the Queen to come into the green wood, and to see how the outlaws live. The King demanded of the Queen and her ladies, if they durst adventure to go into the wood with so many outlaws. Then the Queen said, that if it pleased him, she was content. Then the horns blew till they came to the wood under Shooters Hill, and there was an arbour made of boughs, with a hall and a great chamber and an inner chamber very well made and covered with flowers and sweet herbs, which the King much praised. Then said Robyn hood, Sir, outlaws' breakfast is venison, and therefore you must be content with such fare as we use. Then the King and Queen sat down, and were served with venison and wine by Robyn hood and his men, to their great contentation. Then the King departed and his company, and Robyn hood and his men them conducted . . .

The Scots took the threat rather more seriously. In 1555, the Scottish parliament banned any celebrations that featured Robin Hood, Little John, the Abbot of Unreason and the Queen of the May. Those playing the roles within the royal boroughs were to be banished from the realm, while those choosing them were liable to five years in prison. In the countryside, the punishments were less severe. This did not prevent trouble though. John Knox reported in his *History* that in 1561 in Edinburgh, apprentices and craftsmen gathered 'efter the auld wikkit maner of Robyn Hode' and then

> the rascal Multitude were stirred-up to make a *Robin-Hood*, which enormity was of many years left off and condemned by Statute and Act of Parliament; yet would they not be forbidden, but would disobey and trouble the Town.

The ban on Robin Hood was reconfirmed by Mary Queen of Scots in 1562.

Two more fragments of Robin Hood plays survive from this time. They were appended to the printer William Copland's edition of *A Mery Geste of Robyn Hoode and Hys Lyfe*, published somewhere between 1549 and 1569. However, it was probably printed in 1560 when Copland entered a Robin Hood play on the Stationers' Register. This was the record book of London's Worshipful Company of Stationers which received its royal charter in 1557. By paying a fee of four pence or sixpence, a printer could register the right to publish a particular work. In the introduction to the plays, Copland says they were 'verye proper to be played at the May Games'. It seems that there were numerous different Robin Hood plays organized by parishes and civic bodies all across Britain in the Tudor era.

The first of these surviving fragments is *Robin Hood and the Friar*, which bears comparison to the ballad *Robin Hood and the Curtal Friar*. The play begins with Robin complaining that a 'stoute frere' has beaten him and robbed him. Little John volunteers to go and get the friar bring him to Robin. Fryer Tucke then arrives with three dogs. He and Robin exchange abuse, then blows. Robin sounds his horn to summon his men; the friar whistles. Possibly because of the problem of staging a fight involving dogs, two men called Cut and Bause come on and there is a fight. At the end of it, Robin invites the friar to join him, offering him gold, money and a 'lady free', saying 'And her chapplayn I thee make, To serve her for my sake.'

If the meaning was not clear enough, Fryer Tucke says: 'Here is a huckle duckle, An inch above the buckle', indicating that he wearing an artificial phallus which were commonly worn by comic figures in folk dramas. Then he says that the lady is a 'trul' – or trollop – 'to serve the friar in his lust, A prycker, a prauncer, a tearer of sheets, A wagger of ballocks when other men sleeps'. The play ends with a comic dance, which Fryer Tucke calls a 'daunce in the myre'.

The May games took place out of doors and the play may well have been performed near a river or stream so the part of the story where the friar and Robin carry each other cross the water could be acted out. But this would not always be possible when companies of actors began taking their productions to neighbouring towns. In 1505 there are references to the Robin Hood from Finchampstead arriving in Reading, a journey of 8 miles. That same year the Robin Hood from Henley, 12 miles away, also turned up in Reading. And in 1571, the people of Honiton, Devon, bought a pound of gunpowder to celebrate the arrival of Robin Hood from Colyton, some 6 miles distant.

The second play, *Robin Hood and the Potter*, follows on directly from *Robin Hood and the Friar* in the Copland manuscript and similarly borrows from the earlier ballad. Copland adds the subtitle 'a newe play for to be played on the May games very plesaunte and ful of pastime'. Robin introduces the action, saying:

> Lysten to me my mery men all
> And harke what I shall say
> Of an adventure I shall you tell
> That befell this other daye

He tells of a proud potter who has been travelling the same route for more than seven years and refuses to pay the one penny toll. When Robin asks for someone to go once again and collect the toll, Little John volunteers. Before he can go, the potter's servant boy Jacke appears. Robin smashes his pots and calls his master a cuckold. The potter then appears and denies being a cuckold as 'Wyfe had I never none'. But then, to appease Robin, he offers to sell all his possessions and give Robin half the money. Robin refuses, saying he simply wants the toll. The potter asks why he should have to pay. Robin say: 'For I am Robyn Hode, chiefe governoure under the grene woode tree.'

The potter then challenges Robin to a fight, but Robin calls Little John, who says: 'Be the knave never so stoute, I shall rappe him on the snoute, And put him to flyghte.'

Again much of the entertainment value of the play must have been in the fight scenes rather than the dialogue.

Although Copland and others says that these plays are associated with the May games, they were not necessarily performed on the first of May when they would be competing with dancing around the May tree and other floral dances. The May festivities themselves usually lasted from 1 May to Whitsun. Some authorities record that the Robin Hood plays were being performed 'ere

Pentecost'. Others say they occurred during the 'monthe of May' or when 'May did clad the woods with lustie greene'.

The figure of Robin Hood also appeared in the Mummers plays, where the champion was killed and revived by a doctor, that became popular in England towards the end of the sixteenth century. In a play performed in Shipton under Wychwood in Oxfordshire, a tanner does battle with Robin. Then Little John comes in and is killed. He is revived by the doctor, then Beelzebub make an appearance. This also borrows from the ballad *Robin Hood and the Tanner*, entered in the Stationers' Registry on 17 April 1657. In it, a tanner named Arthur á Bland goes to Sherwood, where he meets Robin Hood who accuses him of poaching. They fight. Robin gets the worst of it and sounds his horn to summon Little John. He tells Little John that Arthur truly is a tanner because he has tanned his hide. Fearing that Arthur will tan his hide too, Little John throws away his staff. They embrace and Arthur joins the Merry Men.

When the London theatres closed during the plague of 1592, Robin Hood was still not part of the professional repertoire. However, he had made an appearance in the history books. John Stow's *Annales of England*, published that year, repeated John Major's assertion that Robin Hood had lived during the reign of Richard I. After that Robin Hood became the hero of popular entertainment. The Robin Hood games make an appearance in George Peele's *The Famous Chronicle of Edward I* in 1593, with the Welsh rebel Lluellen disguising himself as Robin when he tries to take a toll off the King. In 1594, the Stationers' Register lists a play called *Robin Hood and Little John*, but this play has not survived.

In the play *George a Greene* by Robert Greene, Robin plays a secondary role to George who is the pinder of Wakefield. A pinder is a man who captures stray animals. The play was printed in 1599, but it is thought to have been performed as early as 1588–9. George a Greene was already a well-known character. He was a representative of the loyal people of Wakefield, then a burgeoning market town, while Robin, an anti-authority figure, is confined to a minor role. He wears Kendal, not Lincoln, green as Kendal was seen as a centre for insurrection.

In February 1598, the diary of the Elizabethan theatrical impresario Philip Henslowe records that he paid Andrew Munday the enormous sum of £5 to write a Robin Hood play. This was to be *The Downfall of Robert, Earle of Huntington*. There was too much material for one play, however, so on 25 November Henslowe paid Munday and Henry Chettle another £5 to write a sequel, *The Death of Robert, Earle of Huntington*. Chettle received also another 10 shillings for 'the mending of The First Part of Robart Hoode'. The two plays were staged by the Admiral's Men in 1599. They were plainly popular and stayed in the company's repertoire for some time. Both plays were registered with the Stationers' Company on 1 December 1600 and printed the following year.

Munday took Major's idea of Robin being a distressed nobleman and gave it dramatic form. Like Major, he set the action back in the time when Richard I and Prince John were in conflict. But Prince John was not the out-and-out villain he appears in later versions of the story. He is a little hot-headed and is easily dislodged by the return of his brother. He is also portrayed as an enthusiastic admirer of Maid Marian and fights a duel with Friar Tuck of the kind that usually ends with an invitation to join the Merry Men.

In the play, Robert, earl of Huntington, is betrayed by his uncle, the Prior of York, Gilbert de Hood, who owns his debts, and his own steward Warman, who later becomes the Sheriff of Nottingham. Munday was principally a propagandist. He had worked in a semi-official role for the state, both carrying out fact-finding missions and being full-fledged spies. In the play, he sought to appeal directly to the rich and powerful, like his own patron, who was the owner of the Rose theatre and groom of the chamber. Henslowe was a member of the Protestant aristocracy, which had profited from the dissolution of the monasteries and the occupation of Catholic lands, so having Huntington dispossessed by a villainous prior was particularly appealing.

Munday further appealed to Tudor sensibilities by setting Huntington's tale as a play within a play being performed in the court of Henry VIII, who was thought to favour the Robin Hood games. The play opens with a discussion between Henry VIII's former tutor John Skelton, who plays Friar Tuck, and the diplomat Sir John Eltham, who plays Little John. Later, Eltham remarks that he sees none of the traditional elements of the story. Skelton replies that he was asked to write the play by the King, who approved the new material.

During the first scene, Skelton introduces the characters as they come on stage for the first time. First comes Richard 'Cor de Lyon', who is leaving to fight the Pagans in Judea and Palestine. Then comes Robin Hood, who is immediately identified as Robert, earl of Huntington. The plot revolves around Matilda – alias Marian – daughter of Lord Fitzwater. The addition of some love interest was important. The Robin of the ballads was a yeoman and needed no partner. But, as a nobleman, Robert, Earl of Huntington needed a wife to continue the line.

The course of true love is continually thwarted by Prince John's desire for the chaste Matilda and his mother Queen Elinor's for Robin. Robin is further hampered by the machinations of Warman and his uncle, resulting in him becoming an outlaw on the day he is to become betrothed to Marian. The situation then becomes even more complicated thanks to the intervention of Scarlet, Scathlock and Much the miller's son. King Richard then returns and puts everything right. Robin is pardoned and the lovers are reunited.

In *The Death of Robert, Earle of Huntington*, Robin dies a lingering death in the first act after being tricked into swallowing poison by his uncle, the Prior of York, and the mysterious Sir Doncaster. Richard also dies, to be succeeded by King John, who continues his predation of the chaste Marian. Lord Bruce tries to thwart John's intrigues. As a result his wife and son starve to death in the dungeons of Windsor Castle. Marian herself takes refuge in Dunmow Abbey, where she is poisoned by John's evil henchman, Brand, leaving John repentant.

In 1598–9 the Admiral's Men did good business with their two Robin Hood plays. In 1600, they followed up with the ludicrous disguise comedy *Looke About You*, which includes the stage direction 'Enter Robin Hood in Lady Faukenbridge's nightgown, a turban on his head.' It was another hit. The Chamberlain's Men's resident playwright, William Shakespeare, responded with *As You Like It*, which mentions 'Robin Hood of England' in Scene 1. There are two other mentions of Robin Hood in Shakespeare's canon. In 1592–3 he made a reference to 'the bare scalp of Robin Hood's fat friar' in *Two Gentlemen of Verona*, and in 1597 he mentioned 'Robin Hood, Scarlet and John' in *Henry IV, Part 2*, where Justice Silence sings drunkenly to Falstaff a line from what is thought to be the ballad *Robyn Hood and the Pindar of Wakefield*.

By this time, Robin Hood had become a staple of the stage. *Robin Hood's Penn'orths* by William Haughton was listed on the Stationers' Register for 1600–1601, but again it has been lost. Shakespeare's rival Ben Jonson wrote *The Sad Shepherd: A Tale of Robin Hood* around 1635. In it, Robin invited all the shepherds and shepherdesses of the Vale of Belvoir to a feast. Meanwhile Maudlin, the witch of Papplewick, which is in the southern part of Sherwood, disguises herself as Marian. The power of royalty in Jacobean England was so great that, by then, Robin had lost his anti-authoritarian stance and was merely a pastoral figure. By the Restoration in 1660, a radical Robin conceded defeat to the newly re-established royalist authorities in *Robin Hood and His Crew of Soldiers*. The title page of the printed version says that it was performed in Nottingham on the day of Charles II's coronation, 23 April 1661. His father Charles I had raised his standard in Nottingham in 1642 at the beginning of the Civil War. But the city had soon sided with Parliament. With the collapse of the Commonwealth, Nottingham dignitary Francis Harker refused to recant and was executed in 1660. Nottingham's governor, Colonel John Hutchinson, who had been at the Banqueting House on the day of Charles I's execution, was reprieved, but was soon rearrested and died in jail in 1664. The play acted out some of the underlying politics of the post-Civil War period with Robin readily accepting the authority of the crown, despite his outlaw existence, just as previously he accepted the authority of King Richard, after having rebelled against Prince John and the Sheriff of Nottingham.

Music was added to the tale of Robin Hood with *Robin Hood: An Opera* in 1730, *Robin Hood: A New Musical* in 1751 and the comic opera *Robin Hood of Sherwood Forest* in 1782, followed by *Marian* in 1788 and *Merry Sherwood or Harlequin Forester* in 1795. Meanwhile, more ballads had been written, expanding on events in Robin's life or developing the role of other characters. Collections were published from 1777 onwards as interest grew in the medieval, the Gothic and the antiquarian.

In the nineteenth century, Robin Hood went decidedly upmarket. In 1818, John Keats wrote the poem *Robin Hood*. Making an appearance in Sir Walter Scott's *Ivanhoe* the following year, the illiterate young yeoman seems to personify a bucolic English nationalism. Alfred, Lord Tennyson, wrote *The Foresters: Robin Hood and Maid Marian* which, with music by Arthur Sullivan, was produced in New York in 1892, taking advantage of the new interest in the tale of Robin Hood created by Howard Pyle in 1883.

5

THE BANDIT LEADER

In his book *Bandits*, the Marxist historian Eric Hobsbawm identified Robin Hood as 'the international paradigm of social banditry' and gives over an entire chapter to him called 'The Noble Robber'. Hobsbawm compared him with Diego Corrientes (1757–81) from Andalusia, who was seen as a Christ-like figure who robbed from the rich, gave to the poor and killed no one. But after Charles III of Spain offered a hundred gold pieces for his capture, he was betrayed and taken to Seville, where he was hanged, though he had never taken a life. Then there was the robber Juraj Jánošík (1688–1713) who, hidden in the Carpathians, attracted little attention from the authorities. According to legend, he robbed from the nobles and gave to the peasants, and was the subject of numerous songs and tales. A symbol of resistance to oppression, a partisan group took his name during the Slovak National Uprising against the Nazis in 1944.

Hobsbawm identified nine characteristics of the noble robber. First, he must become an outlaw not because of a crime that he has committed, but as the victim of injustice. Or he is being persecuted for some act which the authorities – but not the people – consider criminal. Second, he rights wrongs. Third, he takes from the rich to give to the poor. Fourth, he never kills except in self-defence or out of righteous revenge. Fifth, if he survives his period of outlawry, he returns to the community as an honourable citizen, though he has never really left the people. Sixth, he is admired, aided and supported by his people. Seventh, if he dies, it is invariably through treachery. No decent member of the community would turn against him. Eighth, he possesses mythical qualities of invisibility and invulnerability. Ninth, he is not the enemy of the king or emperor, who is the fount of justice, but only of the local gentry, clergy or other oppressor.

The real Robin Hood – if there was one – fails in most of those criteria. But the mythic one pulls every leaf off the greenwood tree.

Hobsbawm lists some other noble robbers in the Robin Hood mould. There was Angelo Duca, or 'Angiolillo' (1760–84), who became an outlaw after a dispute over stray cattle with one of the field guards of the Duke of Martina. Then there was Pancho Villa (1878–1923) who became a fugitive after killing one of the owners of the estate where he worked in revenge for an assault on his sister. After his first major coup netted him 50,000 pesos, he gave 5,000 pesos to his mother, 4,000 to the families of relatives, and bought a tailor's shop for a man with poor eyesight and a large family. He also hired a man to run the shop, then gave the rest away to the needy.

In Brazil there was the legendary *cangaçeiros*, or bandit, Labarêda – 'The Flame' – who became an outlaw over family honour. Even Jesse James (1847–82) was said to have become an outlaw because he lent a poor widow $800 to meet her debt to a banker, then held up the banker to get his money back. The same story is told of Maté Cosido (born 1897), who robbed trains and banks in the Argentine Chaco, while Luis Pardo (1874–1909), a bandit in Peru, scattered handfuls of silver among the crowd at the fiesta in his home town of Chiquian and distributed sheets, soap, candles, food and other necessities, bought in local shops, to the inhabitants of Llaclla. Even Billy the Kid was a good man in the eyes of Hispanics. He would steal from white European settlers and give it to the Mexicans.

Ch'ao Kai, the bandit leader in the fourteenth-century Chinese classic novel *The Water Margin*, asks after a raid: 'Was no one killed?' When he was told that no one had been hurt, he was pleased and said: 'From this day on, we are not to injure people.' Catalan brigands of the sixteenth and seventeenth centuries killed only in the defence of honour, according to the ballads. The tales of Jesse James and Billy the Kid maintained that they killed only in self-defence or for other just causes, though this seems far from the case in reality. Jesse James was also said to have been a devote Baptist who taught children to sing hymns in school and never to have robbed preachers, widows, orphans or ex-Confederates. However, the idea that these men abstained from unnecessary violence in the violent time they lived in makes them seem virtuous despite their manifest crimes.

Australia's most famous bushranger Ned Kelly (1855–80) stole from the rich and gave to the poor. Already a petty criminal he was driven to become an outlaw when a drunken policeman arrested his mother and jailed her for three years. His gang distributed the proceeds of the bank robberies to relatives, friends and other poor farmers, and burnt the mortgage deeds held by the banks.

Based in the Riverina area of New South Wales, 'Mad Dog' Morgan (1830–65) targeted farmers thought to be hard task masters. During raids, he insisted that employees be fed and given drink. At Burrumbuttock the owner Thomas Gibson was forced to write cheques for his employees totalling some £400.

Bank robber John Dillinger (1903–34) seems an unlikely Robin Hood. He escaped from jail four times with the help of his gang. On one occasion, he carved a wooden gun in his cell at Crown Point, Indiana, to break out from the supposedly escape-proof jail, stealing the sheriff's new car to make his getaway. But, like Robin Hood, he frequently used disguise or deception in his bank heists. He pretended to be a salesman for a company selling alarms, giving him an opportunity to assess a bank's security system. On another occasion his gang pretended to be scouts from a film company looking for locations for a bank-robbery scene. He quickly became a legend. His gang attacked police arsenals, stealing machine guns, pistols, ammunition and bullet-proof vests. He had no compunction when it came to killing policemen, FBI agents and prison guards, but Dillinger planned his robberies meticulously to avoid innocent civilians being killed. If there was an old person in a bank he was about to rob, he would personally escort them out of harm's way. He thought ordinary people were on his side, hitting back at the banks which many blamed for the Great Depression, and he cultivated his image as a gentleman bandit. Once he gave his coat to a bank teller when he took her hostage on a cold winter's day, and he wrote to Henry Ford thanking him for making such reliable getaway cars.

While Dillinger would never open fire in a crowd, the FBI had not such compunction. They gunned down three innocent people in an attempt to capture Dillinger at his hideout in Manitowish Waters, Wisconsin, on 22 July 1934. Two women bystanders were wounded during the FBI's final shoot-out with Dillinger outside the Biograph Theater in the Lincoln Park area of Chicago. He had been betrayed by a prostitute who fingered him to save herself from being deported.

People dipped their handkerchiefs in the pools of Dillinger's blood on the sidewalk as a keepsake. And the legend lives on. Tucson, Arizona, celebrates annual 'Dillinger Days' where there is a re-enactment of his arrest there. On the 75th anniversary of his death, his slaying was re-enacted in Chicago as part of the city's celebration. And, like Robin Hood, John Dillinger has been depicted numerous times in film and on TV.

Around the same time as Dillinger, Bonnie and Clyde were also seen as 'Robin Hood' figures, striking back at the banks which many people found oppressive. According to their biographer, John Neal Phillips, Clyde Barrow (1909–34) became a bank robber not because he sought fame and fortune, but to revenge himself on the Texas prison system for the abuses he suffered while serving time. The other members of the Barrow gang said Bonnie Parker (1910–1934) never fired a gun, though she was an accomplished writer whose poems *Suicide Sal* and *The Story of Bonnie and Clyde* helped secure their legendary status. Between 1932 and 1934, there were several incidents where the Barrow Gang kidnapped lawmen or robbery victims, releasing them far away and giving them the money to get back home. Stories of these encounters consolidated their reputation and the couple were both adored and reviled by the public. Notoriously, the Barrow Gang would not hesitate to shoot anybody, civilian or lawman, who got in their way. However, while Clyde had been careless with people's lives early his career, when he was with Bonnie he confined his murders to police officers. They escaped numerous brushes with the law. Barrow saw no problem taking on the lawmen's machine guns with his Browning automatic rifle capable of firing a twenty-round clip of .30-06 (7.62x63mm) armour-piercing shells in less than three seconds.

In January 1934, Clyde finally took his revenge on the Texas Department of Corrections by organizing a breakout from Eastham prison farm. This brought the wrath of the authorities down on their heads. The famous Texas Ranger Captain Frank A. Hamer was brought out of retirement to track them down. After the murder of several more officers, Bonnie and Clyde were gunned down by the police in an ambush in Bienville Parish, Louisiana. They have been portrayed on TV and in movies, including the 1967 film *Bonnie and Clyde*, starring Faye Dunaway and Warren Beatty, as romantic rebels.

In remote areas of the Balkans, Corsica, Calabria or Sicily, which are untroubled by authority or the law, bandits were not only tolerated and protected, but became leading members of the community. Kota Christov of Roulia, who lived in the depths of Macedonia in the late nineteenth century, was the most feared bandit leader of the region at the time. But he was also the leading citizen of his village, running a shop and an inn, and providing other public services. On behalf of the villagers, he resisted the landowners, who were mainly Albanian, as well as the Turkish officials who came to requisition food for their soldiers and policemen. He was a devout Christian who knelt before the shrine at the Byzantine monastery of the Holy Trinity after each of his exploits and particularly deplored the wanton killing of Christians – except, presumably, Albanians. While supporting himself by brigandry, he allied himself first with the Turks, then with a Macedonian revolutionary organization, and finally with the Greeks in an attempt to defend the rights of his people against injustice and oppression.

The Robin Hood of Calabria was Giuseppe Musolino – better known as Brigante Musolini or the King of Aspromonte. He became an outlaw after being falsely accused of murder and imprisoned. He escaped to take revenged on those who had given false testimony against him. During his life of crime he helped the peasants, gave large sums of stolen money to monasteries and churches, and kept King Victor Emanuel informed by letter of the need for local reforms. The women of San Stefano would pray for him:

> Musolino is innocent.
> They had condemned him unjustly;
> Oh Madonna, oh St Joseph
> Let him always be under your protection
> Oh Jesus, oh my Madonna,
> Keep him from harm
> Now and forever, so let it be.

On his way to seek a pardon from Victor Emanuel, he was captured and sent to prison, where he died insane at the age of 79.

The gaucho brigands of Argentina, often veterans of the political wars of the nineteenth century, were also venerated. Their graves, usually decorated in the colours of their party, were said to work miracles.

While Robin Hood died after being betrayed by his relative, the Prioress of Kirklees, Jesse James was betrayed by Robert Ford, and Billy the Kid by Pat Garrett. According to legend the Carpathian bandit Oleksa Dovbush (1700–45) was betrayed by his mistress, Erzika, or her husband. In fact, he was shot in the back by Salvatore Dzvinka, a peasant he had aided.

The legendary Sicilian bandit Salvatore Giuliano (1922–50), who became an outlaw because he resisted a revenue man he was too poor to bribe, was killed by his lieutenant Gaspare Pisciotta, who had been promised a pardon. Pisciotta died in jail four years later, after drinking a cup of tea laced with strychnine. Angiolillo and Diego Corrientes were also betrayed.

While these men may not meet the Hobsbawm criteria of invisibility – many of them sought publicity – they were famously illusive, blending in with the people who surrounded them or hiding away in remote regions. Some, in folk lore at least, never died. Pasquale Romano, formerly a sergeant in the Bourbon army, was the leader of a band of brigands that infested the greater part of Puglia in southeast Italy. Although he was killed in 1863, people still believe he roams the countryside.

Francisco Gonzáles Ríos – 'El Pernales' (1879–1907) – was driven to banditry by hunger and the death of his father at the hands of the Spanish authorities. He joined a band called the Children of Glory. After he was shot down by the Guardia Civil, the story was that he had escaped to Mexico. Likewise it was said that Jesse James survived being shot in the back by gang member Robert Ford and went to live in California. Despite Robin Hood's evident death in Kirklees, he appeared all over England for many years after.

Some southern Italian brigands thought themselves invulnerable because they wore amulets blessed by the Pope or the King. Others believed themselves to be under the protection of the Virgin. In southern Peru, they were protected by Our Lady of Luren. Local holy men bestow their protection on bandits in Brazil, while outlaws in southern Asia depend on magic. The *Aheriya dacoits* (armed gangs) of Uttar Pradesh consulted omens before their robberies, though the bravest leaders would forgo this. And Lampião (1897–1938), who terrorized northeast Brazil in the 1920s and 1930s, was treated by a *feiticeiro* or witch doctor called Master Macumba who, according to a folksong, used the strongest African magic to make him invulnerable to the knife or gun. But the magician advised him, in case of special need, to appeal to 'St Legs, St Vigilant, St Rifle, St Suspicious, St Lookout'. Lampião – which means 'Oil Lamp' in Portuguese – was driven into banditry after he had taken vengeance on the police who had killed his father. After nineteen years on the run, he was betrayed by a follower and proved all to vulnerable to machine-gun fire.

Robin Hood did not resort to magic. But he did pray to the Virgin Mary, though he had little time for the established Church. Although he regularly lost in fights, his opponents generally saw the rightness of his cause and accept his invitation to join the Merry Men.

Like other noble robbers, Robin does not challenge the authority of the King, who is sometimes misled by treacherous counsellors such as the Sheriff of Nottingham. However, when the King meets Robin face to face, he recognizes Robin's virtue, pardons him and, in some versions of the tale, takes him into service. The career of José María Pelagio Hinojosa Cobacho (known as 'El Tempranillo' or the Early One, 1805–33) – the Robin Hood of Andalucía – followed much the same path. José Maria was driven into banditry by the poverty that followed the Napoleonic invasion of Spain in the early nineteenth century. He is said to have killed his first man at the age of thirteen after an attack on his family. Hiding out in the Sierra Morena along the Portuguese border, he established his own gang based in a cave near the Despeñaperros pass, the main route into Andalucía from the north. There he levied a tithe on rich travellers, even collecting his payment in broad daylight. El Tempranillo quickly became famous for his charm, once telling a woman traveller, 'Ah, señora! A hand so beautiful as yours does not need adornments!' while relieving the blushing traveller of her rings and other jewellery. Then he kissed her hand and bid her a safe onward journey. He also acquired a reputation for redistributing his ill-gotten gains among the poor, making him a cult figure throughout Andalucía and beyond. He once announced that, while the king may rule Spain, El Tempranillo ruled the sierra – giving him his nickname King of the Sierra Morena. At one point, Don Vincente Quesada, Captain General of Andalucía's armed forces, was so frustrated at his inability to catch the outlaw that he offered a reward of 6,000 reales for El Tempranillo, dead or alive. El Tempranillo responded by taunting Don Vincente. After his wife died in childbirth in 1831, El

Tempranillo rode into the mountain village of Grazalema, north-west of Ronda, accompanied by 50 horsemen, to have his son baptized in the village's Nuestra Señora de la Aurora church, while the authorities looked on helplessly.

The English travel writer John Ford wrote: 'When Fernando VII was the king of Spain and José Maria was the love of Andalucía.' The artist John Frederic Lewis produced a portrait depicting him as a small man on an equally small horse, with dark hair, blue eyes, a large mouth and thin pointed nose, dressed in a fine shirt and a velvet jacket with silver buttons and leather bindings.

El Tempranillo's daring broad daylight hold-ups, and his increasing popularity among the general pubic, eventually forced King Fernando VII to offer him a pardon in August 1832, provided he work for the state. Don José was made commander in chief of the *Escuadrón Franco de Protección y Seguridad Pública de Andalucía* – 'the free squadron for the protection and public security of Andalucía'. He had under his command 60 mounted guards who wore a uniform similar to that of the Spanish army. This was eleven years before the establishment of Spain's Guardia Civil in 1844.

The bandit turned policeman was fatally wounded in a shoot-out while attempting to arrests the bandit El Barbarello, from Estepa, on the road between Alameda and Mollina on 22 September 1833. He was taken to the Parador de San Antonio in calle Granada in Alameda, and died the following day. Despite his years of banditry, El Tempranillo left little to his orphaned son – just two small houses, two horses and a few reales borrowed from friends. However, his right-hand man, Luis Borrego, became mayor of the township of Benamejí, after he gave up brigandry.

While these latter-day bandits have often been compared with Robin Hood, the tale of Robin Hood itself borrows from earlier figures and two near contemporaries – legendary Fulk FitzWarin and Eustace the Monk.

6

FULK FITZWARIN

The FitzWarin family were landowners and from around 1145 to 1315 they were a leading family in the Welsh Marches. When Henry I died in 1135, the first Fulk FitzWarin (died 1171) sided with Henry's daughter Matilda against Henry's nephew Stephen who usurped the throne. As a reward he received the manor of Alveston in Gloucester from Matilda's son Henry Plantagenet, who became Henry II of England in 1154. It seems he was also given land at Whittington in Shropshire, which had been held by the Peverel family during Stephen's reign, and Whadborough in Leicestershire.

His eldest son Fulk (II) FitzWarin (died 1197) made an advantageous marriage and increased the family's land-holding around Whittington. Fulk (III) FitzWarin (died

1258), sought to hold on to Whittington, even paying a fine of £100 levied on the manor. But when King John came to the throne in 1199 he gave Whittington to the son and then the grandsons of Roger of Powys. Aggrieved, Fulk led a small rebellion against the King. He had 52 followers, including his three brothers, some of the family's tenants and the younger sons of many of Shropshire's landed families. When the King sent Hubert de Burgh with 100 knights to put down the rebellion, Fulk fell back on guerrilla tactics. The King was forced to settle. On 11 November 1203 Fulk and his followers were pardoned and, after paying 200 marks, he took over Whittington Castle.

In 1215, Fulk broke with the King again, siding with the barons, but was reconciled the following year, after the signing of Magna Carta. But the King remained suspicious and gave him only restricted permission to improve the defences of his castles. Consequently Whittington and Fulk's castle at Alberbury were seized by the Welsh in 1223, and they held on to them until 1226. After 1228, Fulk became a trusted courtier of Henry III.

Fulk (III) lived to a great age and it seems that, for the final seven years of his life, he was blind. His son, Fulk (IV) FitzWarin, managed his affairs until finally inheriting his estates. He supported Henry III in his war against the barons and was drowned in a stream at the battle of Lewes on 14 May 1264. His lands were seized by Simon de Montfort. After de Montfort was killed at the Battle of Evesham in August 1265, they were held by Hamon L'Estrange until Fulk (V) FitzWarin was old enough to inherit.

The story of the FitzWarin family was preserved in the romance *Fouke le Fitz Waryn*. This exists as a fourteenth-century manuscript, though the story was probably written between 1258 and 1265. It conflates the story of Fulk (I) and Fulk (II) and concentrates on the remarkable career of Fulk (III). According to the tale, as a young boy, Fulk (III) is sent to the court of Henry II, where he is brought up with the future King John. One day, Fulk and John are alone in a room playing chess. Suddenly, John picks up the chess board and hits Fulk with it. In response Fulk kicks John in the chest. As John goes flying backwards, he hits his head and passes out. Terrified that he may have killed the prince, Fulk rubs John's temples until he comes round. John then runs to his father, Henry II, and tells him what Fulk has done. But after hearing Fulk's side of the story, the King says that John deserved what he had got and has him thrashed. This creates a rift between the two boys.

When John's brother Richard comes to the throne, he holds the FitzWarin family in high esteem and knights all the men in the family. They seek honour fighting abroad and take part in every joust and tournament. When Sir Fulk (II) dies, his lands are given to Sir Fulk (III) and when Richard goes off to fight in Palestine, he puts Sir Fulk (III) in charge of the Welsh March. However, when John becomes King, he is approached by Moris, son of Roger of Powys, who brings him a prize falcon. John then makes Sir Moris warden of the March. As he rises in John's favour, Moris asks the King for Whittington. John sees an opportunity to revenge himself on Fulk for the thrashing he had received as a boy and grants Sir Moris the manor in return for a fee of £100 cash.

A knight nearby overhears the conversation and rushes to tell Fulk. Sir Fulk and his four brothers then go to the King and argue that, under common law, the lands belong to Fulk and offer him the £100 fee. But the King says that he has already given the lands to Sir Moris.

Sir Moris then turns on Sir Fulk.

'Sir Knight, you are very foolish to challenge my lands,' he says. 'If you say that you have right to Whittington you lie. Were it not for the King's presence, I would prove it upon your body.'

Before any more words are exchanged, Fulk's brother Sir William punches Sir Moris in the face. The two are quickly separated and Sir Fulk says to the King: 'Sire, you are my liege lord, and I have become bound to you by fealty since I have been in your service, and because I hold lands from you. In return you ought to afford me reasonable support, but you fail me both in reason and in common law. Never has a good King denied law in his court to his free tenants; therefore, I renounce my allegiance to you.'

That said, he leaves the court.

Fulk and his brothers quickly arm themselves. Half a league (about a mile and a half) from court, they are confronted by 15 well-armed knights, the King's champions, who order them to return. When they refuse, the knights say they have promised the King that he should have their heads.

'Fair sirs,' says Fulk, 'you were very foolish when you promised to give what you could not get.'

A battle ensues. Four of the King's most valiant knights are killed outright. All the others are grievously wounded – except one, who flees. When he returns to court, the King asks if FitzWarin has been taken prisoner.

'Not at all,' the knight replies, 'nor was he even injured. He and all his companions have escaped, and all of our men, excepting myself, were slain. I alone escaped with great difficulty.'

The King then asks where Gyrart de France, Pierre of Avignon and Sir Amys le Marchys are. The knight answered, 'Slain, sire.'

Then the ten wounded knights arrived. They are on foot as Fulk had made off with their chargers. Some of these knights have lost their noses, some their chins. They are a piteous sight. The King is so angry that he swears a great oath that he will take revenge on them and all their lineage.

Fulk and his brother and cousins flee to Brittany. King John takes over the rest of Fulk's lands. But when John attacks his family, Fulk and his followers have little choice except to return to England. Travelling by night and hiding by day, they arrive in Shropshire. They lay in wait in Babbins Wood near Whittington for Sir Moris. However, one of Moris's servants sees them. Moris assembles a force of 30 horsemen with 500 on foot. When they reach the wood, Fulk and his men rush out to confront them. Moris is wounded in the shoulder. Then when many of his knights and foot soldiers lay dead, he flees. Fulk catches up with him a short way out his castle and takes a swing at his helmet. He misses and his sword hits the saddle of his charger. Morgan, the son of one of Moris's knights, comes out of the castle and hits Fulk in the leg with a crossbow bolt, preventing him finishing off Moris.

Sir Moris complains to King John that Fulk has returned to England and attacked him. John is angry and sends 100 knights to seek out Fulk. Meanwhile, Fulk and his men hide in Braydon Forest in Wiltshire.

One day, a number of merchants come through the forest, carrying expensive cloths, furs, spices and dresses for the King and Queen. They are escorted by 24 foot-soldiers. Fulk sends his brother John to intercept them. He invites them to come and meet his master in the forest. A man-at-arms comes forward and strikes John with his sword. John hits him on the head and he falls senseless to the ground. Then Fulk arrives. After a fight, he takes them into the forest.

When Fulk learns that the goods they are carrying are destined for the King, he asks: 'Sir merchants, if you lose this property, on whom will the loss fall? Tell me the truth.'

'Sir, if we lose it through our cowardice, or by our own carelessness, we ourselves are responsible,' they say, 'but if we lose it otherwise, by danger of the sea, or by force, the loss will fall upon the King.'

When he hears this, he begins dividing the goods among his followers. The merchants are given a feast. Afterwards Fulk sends them on their way, asking them to salute the King in the name of Fulk FitzWarin and thank him for the fine clothes. Hearing this, John is furious and offers a reward of £1,000, along with all of Fulk's land, to anyone who will bring in the outlaw, dead or alive.

Fulk moves to the forests of Kent where he hides with his men. One day he meets a messenger who is singing merrily. He wears a garland of red roses around his head. Fulk buys them for 20 shillings, twice what they are worth. When the messenger arrives in Canterbury, he meets the 100 knights that are hunting for Fulk and tells them he has just met him. The knights then round up enough men to surround the entire forest.

Alerted by the sound of hunting horns, Fulk and his men ride out to confront the 100 knights. In the first charge, Fulk's men kill Gilbert de Mountferrant, Jordan de Colchester, and many other knights. But then other knights, squires, foot-soldiers join the battle. Many are killed. But after his brother John receives a bad head wound, Fulk decides to return into the safety of the forest. They seek sanctuary in a nearby abbey. The porter sees them coming and runs to shut the gates. But Fulk's youngest brother Alan is very tall and gets over the wall. The porter flees. Alan runs after him, knocks him down and grabs his keys. Then he unlocks the gate and lets his brothers in. Fulk grabs a monk's habit and puts it on. He takes a large staff and goes out of the gate, limping and using the staff as a crutch. Soon he meets the knights, followed by a great rabble.

One of the knights asks: 'Old monk, have you seen any armed knights pass here?'

'Indeed, sir,' says Fulk, 'and may God repay them for all the mischief that they have done.'

'What have they done to you?'

'I could not get out of their way quickly enough,' says Fulk, 'and they had their horses trample over me.'

'You will be well avenged this very day,' says the knight.

They take off at great speed, leaving the abbey far behind them. At some distance, they are followed by Sir Gyrard de Malfee and 10 knights. Seeing Fulk, Sir Gyrard says: 'Here is a fat and burly monk. He has a belly big enough to hold two gallons of cabbage.'

Without a word, Fulk strikes Sir Gyrard such a blow with his staff that the knight falls senseless to the ground. Fulk's brothers rush out of the abbey and subdued the 10 knights. After tying up their prisoners, they take their horses and ride non-stop until they come to Higford in

Shropshire, where John's wounds are tended and given time to heal.

At Higford a messenger arrives from the Archbishop of Canterbury, Hubert Walter, who wants to speak to Fulk urgently. So Fulk takes his men back to Kent and hides them in the forest where they had been before. Then he and his brother William disguise themselves as merchants and go into Canterbury to speak to the Archbishop.

Fulk's brothers, his principal followers, are, like Robin's, John, Alan and Will.

'You no doubt know that my brother Sir Theobald Walter is dead,' says the Archbishop. 'Before his death he married Dame Matilda de Caus, a very rich lady, and the fairest in all England. King John himself desires her for her beauty, and she has difficulty guarding herself from him . . . My dear friend Fulk, I ask you to take her for your wife, with my blessing.'

According to the poem, as well as being wicked without conscience, ill-tempered and hated by all good people, King John was lustful. Whenever he heard of any fair lady or damsel, he wished to have her immediately, either by entrapping her with a promise or gift, or by ravishing her by force. It did not matter whether she was the wife or daughter of an earl or a baron. That was why many great lords of England turned against him.

When Fulk meets Matilda, he sees for himself how beautiful and virtuous she is. She has an excellent reputation, as well as lands, castles and cities in Ireland. So he marries her. After two days, Fulk leaves her in Canterbury under the protection of the Archbishop and returns to his men in the forest. When he tells them what he has done, they laugh at him, calling him 'husband', and ask whether he is going to keep his fair lady in a castle or in the forest. Besides joking, they take every opportunity to do serious mischief to the King, but hurt no one other than the King and those who are openly their enemies.

At the time there was a knight named Pieres de Bruvyle, who had gathered a gang around him. They go around the country, killing and robbing merchants and other decent people under the assumed name of Fulk FitzWarin. Consequently the real Fulk and his men are blamed for things they have not done and their reputation is blackened. As a result he dares not stay too long in one place. He is frequently pursued by the King and his men and, to put them off his trail, he has his horses shod with the shoes on backwards.

Fulk has a friend named Robert Fitz-Sampson. He is a very rich man who live in the Scottish March. One night, as Fulk is approaching Robert Fitz-Sampson's court, he can hear people talking and hears his name mentioned often. While his men remain outside, Fulk enters the courtyard and makes his way into the great hall. Once inside he can see Pieres and his knights eating supper. They are wearing masks and those serving the meal kneel before Sir Pieres and call him Sir Fulk.

Nearby Robert Fitz-Sampson and his wife are laid on the floor, bound with ropes. Alone, Fulk steps forward with his sword drawn, saying if anyone is bold enough to move a hand or a foot, he swears he will cut them to pieces.

'Now,' says Fulk, 'which of you here calls himself Fulk?'

'I am that knight,' says Pieres. 'I am Fulk.'

'Well, Sir Fulk,' Fulk shouts, 'you had better move quickly. Tie up all your companions tightly. If you do not, you will be the first to lose your head.'

Pieres unties Robert Fitz-Sampson and his wife and ties up his men instead. Then Fulk cuts their heads off. He says to Pieres: 'You recreant knight, you who called yourself Fulk, you are a cowardly liar. I am Fulk, and you will now pay dearly for having falsely caused me to be charged with theft.'

And he cuts off Pieres' head. Then he called his men to join him for supper.

Afterwards Fulk and his men return to the forest. Then he sends John de Rampaigne, who is skilled at juggling and minstrelsy, to Whittington to perform before Moris Fitz-Roger and see what he is up to.

John disguises himself by dressing in tatters and taking a herb that makes his face swollen and discoloured. Moris asks where he is from. John replied Scotland.

'What news do you have from there?' asks Moris.

'Sir, I know none, other than the recent death of Sir Fulk FitzWarin,' says John. 'He was killed in a robbery at the house of Sir Robert Fitz-Sampson.'

John is rewarded for this news with a silver cup. But some of Moris's household mock him for his swollen face. John raises his staff and gives one of them such a blow that his brains fly into the middle of the room.

John returns to Fulk and tells him that Sir Moris, as keeper of the March, is planning to move 15 knights and his entire household to the castle of Shrewsbury the very next day. On his way, he meets Fulk and is quickly despatched by him and his knights.

Then Fulk goes to Rhuddlan in Flintshire to speak to Llewelyn the Great, Prince of Gwynned (1199–1240). He had also been brought up in the court of Henry II, alongside Fulk and his brothers, and he is married to Joan, King John's sister.

'Sir, I cannot have peace with the King no matter what I do,' says Fulk. 'I have, therefore, come to make peace with you.'

'Truly, I grant and give you my peace,' says the Prince. 'The King of England doesn't know how to have peace with you, or me, or any other.'

'Sir,' says Fulk, 'many thanks, for I trust much in you and in your great loyalty. But since you have granted me your peace, I must tell you something else. Moris Fitz-Roger is dead. I have killed him.'

Moris was Llewelyn's cousin and the Prince becomes very angry. If he had not just given his peace to Fulk, he says, he would have had him drawn and hanged. Then Princess Joan steps in and they put aside any ill will and embrace each other. Fulk then reconciles Llewelyn with Gwenwynwyn, who owns much of Powys.

King John is at Winchester when the news arrives that Fulk has killed Moris Fitz-Roger. Then he learns that Fulk is staying with Prince Llewelyn, his own brother-in-law.

'By Saint Mary, I am the King,' cries John. 'I rule England. I am duke of Anjou and Normandy, and the whole of Ireland is under my lordship. Yet I cannot find a single man in all my jurisdiction who, no matter how much I offer to give, will avenge me for the damage and the disgrace which Fulk has done me. But you can be certain that I will not desist until I avenge myself upon this Prince.'

John assembles an army at Shrewsbury, while Fulk waits with 30,000 men at Bala Castle in Pennlyn, Merionethshire. Fulk knows that, to reach him, the King must cross the ford at Gymele where the road goes through a very narrow pass, enclosed by marshes and woods. He and Gwenwynwyn dig a ditch and build a palisade across the highway there. When King John arrives at the ford, he sees 10,000 armed knights beyond. Fulk and Gwenwynwyn attack. When Gwenwynwyn is wounded, they withdraw behind the palisade. From there, Fulk's men cut down the King's troops with crossbows and spears. That evening, King John is forced to retire to Shrewsbury after losing many men.

Llewelyn goes on to take Ruyton-of-the-Eleven-Towns in Shropshire from Sir John Lestrange, one of the few to have remained loyal to King John. Llewelyn then restores Whittington to Fulk, and also gives him Ystrat Marchell in Montgomeryshire and Dinorben in Denbighshire. After thanking the Prince, Fulk and his men go to Whittington to repair the castle there.

The King gives Lestrange 10,000 knights under Sir Henry de Audley to take back Whittington. Fulk has just 700 men there, including Welsh knights and foot soldiers. Nevertheless, he rides out to meet the King's army. In the first engagement, Fulk slices through Sir John's helmet, scarring him for life. But Fulk's brothers Alan and Philip the Red are wounded. Enraged, Fulk slashes out killing all those around him, but they are so greatly outnumbered that they have to flee back to Whittington.

In the battle Fulk's cousin Sir Audulph de Bracy has been knocked from his horse and taken as a prisoner back to Shrewsbury. There King John threatens to have Sir Audulph hung, drawn and quartered as a traitor and a thief. Audulph defends himself, saying that neither he nor any of his kinsmen are traitors.

Seeing Fulk's concern over his cousin, John de Rampaigne volunteers to go to King John and bring back news of Sir Audulph. This time he dresses himself in fine clothes and stains his hair, face and body jet black. At Shrewsbury, he kneels before the King who asks where he is from.

'Sire,' says John, 'I am an Ethiopian minstrel.'

'What do they say of me in foreign realms?'

'Sire,' says he, 'you are the most renowned King in the whole of Christendom. It is your great renown that explains my visit to your court' – adding *sotto voce* that John is renowned more for his wickedness than his goodness.

John spends the rest of the day entertaining the court with his tabor and other instruments. When the King has gone to bed, Sir Henry de Audley, who has been drinking, sends for Sir Audulph, saying that he should at least have a pleasant night before his death as the King intends to have him executed the next day.

When Sir Audulph arrives, John sings a song which he knows Sir Audulph will recognize. Sir Audulph looks at the minstrel and sees through the blackened face his old friend John. When Sir Henry asks for more drink, John serves everyone, deftly sprinkling a powder into their cups. Sir Henry's men are soon unconscious. John and Sir Audulph escape through a window over the Severn and make their way back to Whittington.

It is only then that King John learns that Fulk has married Matilda de Caus. He orders her to be seized, but she finds sanctuary in a church where she gives birth to a daughter.

Later Fulk and his men enter Canterbury under cover of darkness. From there, they take Matilda to Higford. When she is pregnant again, she takes refuge in the church of Our Lady at Shrewsbury, where she gives birth to another daughter. Subsequently, on her next pregnancy,

Matilda has a son. He is born in the Welsh mountains and baptized in a stream flowing from the Maiden's Well. This is Fulk (IV).

When the King realizes that there is no way to avenge himself upon Fulk, nor disgrace or take his wife, he sends a letter to his own brother-in-law, Prince Llewelyn. He promises to return all the lands that his ancestors have taken from the Prince in return for Fulk's body. When the Prince shows his wife the letter, she immediately sends a full report of it to Fulk, who fears he might be betrayed. Lodging Matilda back in Canterbury under the protection of the Archbishop, Fulk and his men flee to France.

Fulk then gets involved in all sorts of acts of derring-do. Nearing Paris, he sees a tournament attended by King Philip of France. The French knight Sir Druz de Montbener invites the English knights to join in. When the King sees Sir Fulk in full battle dress, he says to Sir Druz de Montbener: 'Take heed, sir, for it is quite obvious that this English knight is very valiant.'

'Sire,' replies Sir Druz, 'there is not a knight in all the world whom I would not dare to take on man-to-man, either on horse or on foot.'

On the first tilt, Fulk's lance wounds Sir Druz in the shoulder and knocks him off his horse. A second knight's lance pierces Fulk's shield, but again he knocks the man from his saddle. King Philip then stops the fight.

'English knight,' he says. 'A blessing upon you, for you have done exceedingly well.'

The King asks Fulk his name. Fulk says it is 'Amys del Boys'.

'Sir Amys,' says the King, 'do you know Fulk FitzWarin, of whom so much good is spoken everywhere?'

'Yes, sire, I have seen him quite often,' says Fulk.

'And what is his stature?'

'Sire, he is about the same height as I am.'

'That he may well be, for you are both valiant men.'

Fulk travels all over France to jousts and tournaments. He is held in the highest esteem and praised everywhere he goes for his courage, chivalry and prowess.

When King John finally learns that Fulk is staying in France, he sends a letter to King Philip requesting him to expel his mortal enemy Fulk FitzWarin from his household. The King of France replies that there is no knight of that name in his retinue. But when Fulk hears the news he goes directly to see the King of France to tell him he is leaving. Philip begs him to stay. Fulk says that he has heard news that compels him to leave.

'Sir Amys de Boys,' says the King. 'I believe that you are in fact Fulk FitzWarin.'

'Yes, my lord, I am indeed.'

'Stay here with me,' the King begs, 'and I will give you richer lands than any you have ever had in England.'

'With due respect, my lord,' Fulk replies, 'a man who cannot reasonably hold those which are his own by right heritage is unworthy to receive lands as a gift from someone else.'

At the coast, Fulk meets a sailor named Mador of Mont de Russie.

'Mador,' says Fulk, 'yours is a very perilous trade. Tell me, brother, how did your father die?'

Mador says that his father had drowned at sea.

'And how did your grandfather die?'

'In the same way.'

'How's about your great-grandfather?'

'In the same manner, as did all my relations, to the fourth generation, as far as I know,' says Mador.

'Truly,' says Fulk, 'it is very foolhardy of you to venture out to sea.'

'Why indeed, sir? Every creature shall have the death that is destined for him,' says the sailor. 'Now then, if you please, answer my question. Where did your father die?'

'In his bed, of course.'

'Where did your grandfather die?'

'In the same place.'

'And your great-grandfather?'

'Certainly, all of my lineage, as far as I know, died in their beds.'

'Assuredly, sir,' says Mador, 'since all your kindred have died in their beds, I am much astonished that you dare go near any bed.'

Fulk commissions Mador to build him a ship and they set sail for England. As they draw near the coast, a well-armed vessel approaches them. A knight on board calls out to Mador: 'Mariner, who owns the ship which you are steering, and what is her provenance? For it is an unfamiliar vessel in these waters.'

'The ship is my own, sir,' says Mador.

'By my faith!' says the knight. 'That is not so. You are thieves. I know it by the quartered sail, which bears the arms of Fulk FitzWarin. He must be on board the ship, and this very day I will deliver his body up to King John.'

'You will do no such thing,' says Fulk. 'But if you want some of our provisions, you are welcome to them.'

'I would prefer to take all of you,' he says, 'and whatever belongs to you.'

Mador lets out his sails and steers his ship directly at the other vessel, hitting it amidships. The sea pours into its hold. Fulk and his men immediately board and plunder it before it breaks in two and sinks.

For a year Fulk continues sailing up and down the coast of England, seizing what he can of the King's property, but leaving everyone else unharmed. Then they set sail for Scotland, but a strong west wind carries them well past their destination. A beautiful island appears in the distance. Fulk and his four brothers, along with their cousins Audulph and Baldwin, go ashore to find food. They meet a young shepherd who leads them to a cavern, then he sounds a horn, to summons his servant he says.

Six fierce-looking peasants arrive. Fulk immediately suspects there is going to be trouble. But the peasants go into another chamber and return dressed in rich green clothing with shoes ornamented in gold. They bring out four chessboards with pieces made of gold and silver, and invite their guests to play. John, Alan, William, Philip the Red, Audulph and Baldwin all lose one after the other, but Fulk refuses to play.

'You will either play chess or wrestle me,' says the peasant. 'You have no other choice.'

'Since I am forced either to wrestle or play chess despite myself,' says Fulk. 'I choose instead to play the game I know best.'

Fulk draws his sword, and strikes the peasant such a blow that his head flies into the middle of the room. A second, then a third meet a similar fate. Then Fulk and his men finish off the rest of them and search the cavern. In a nearby chamber Fulk finds an old woman sitting with a horn which she has put to her mouth, but does not have the strength to blow. Fulk asks her what would happen if she blew the horn. She says that if the horn were blown help would come immediately.

In another chamber, Fulk finds seven beautiful damsels. When they see Fulk they throw themselves on their knees and cry for mercy.

'Sir, I am the daughter of Aunflor of Orkney,' says one.

She had been out at sea with her handmaidens and an armed escort when they had been attacked by the old woman's seven sons. They had killed her escort and brought her and her handmaidens to the island.

'Against our consent they have repeatedly ravished our bodies, and heaven is our witness,' she says. 'Wherefore we pray, in the name of the God, for you to save us.'

Fulk's men plunder the island, with Fulk taking a rich coat of mail that he keeps for the rest of his life. They load their ship with provisions, treasure and get the damsels on board. Then, when Fulk's men have armed themselves, he sounds the old woman's horn. Other pirates come running from all over the island. Fulk and his men kill more than two hundred of them before setting sail.

After returning the damsels to the Orkneys, they sail to the seven islands of the ocean, including Ireland, Gotland, Norway, Denmark and Sweden, where nothing dwells except for horned serpents and venomous beasts with heads like mastiffs that have been driven from Ireland by St Patrick. A tempest then carries them through ice-filled waters to Carthage, where Fulk rescues a duke's daughter from a dragon. The duke offers Fulk his daughter's hand in marriage. Fulk says he would have accepted had he not already been married and a Christian.

Finally, they return to England. When they arrive at Dover, Fulk tells Mador to keep the ship in a safe location nearby. Then he and his men go inland. They learn that King John is at Windsor and hide out in Windsor Forest, which Fulk knows well. Hearing a horn sounding, Fulk realizes that the King is going out for a hunt and sets out to challenge him alone.

On his way, Fulk meets an old charcoal-burner, dressed in black. Fulk asks him to give him his clothes in exchange for 10 besants (Byzantine gold coins). When King John and three knights arrive, they find Fulk tending the charcoal-burner's fire. Seeing the King, Fulk falls to his knees, to the amusement of the knights.

'My good peasant,' says the King, 'did you see a deer pass this way?'

'Yes, my lord, some time ago,' says Fulk.

'Where is it now?'

'Sire, I can lead you where I saw it.'

'Go on and we will follow you,' says the King.

Fulk leads the King to a good place to shoot from – the King prides himself on being a very good bowman.

'My lord,' says Fulk, 'would you like me to go into the thicket and get the animal to come out this way?'

'Yes, indeed,' says the King.

So Fulk disappears into the thick of the forest and summons his men. Together they rush out of the thicket and capture the King.

'Now, sire,' says Fulk, 'I have you in my power at last. Shall I pass such sentence on you as you would on me if you had taken me?'

Fulk swears that the King should die for the great damage he has inflicted on him and on many other good Englishmen. The King trembles with fear, cries for mercy and, in God's name, begs for his life. On earth he pledges to restore Fulk's entire inheritance and whatever he has taken from his friends, pledging his friendship and peace for ever.

Back at his palace, King John says that his oath had been made under duress and he has no intention of keeping it. He orders his men to go out and capture the felons while they are still in Windsor Forest.

Sir James of Normandy, the King's cousin, asks to be in the vanguard with his 15 knights as the English nobles are Fulk's cousins and more likely to be loyal to him than to the King. Randolph, the earl of Chester, protests at this and would have punched Sir James in the face had the Earl Marshal not restrained him.

'Let us go after Sir Fulk,' says the Earl Marshal. 'Then the King will see for himself who might be holding back for reasons of family ties.'

John de Rampaigne had overheard all this and reports them back to Fulk, who concludes that he has no choice but to fight. So his men arm themselves and go out to take on Sir James and his 15 knights, who wear white armour and ride white steeds. In a fierce battle they kill all Sir James's men except for four, who are seriously wounded. Sir James himself is taken prisoner. Fulk and his men put on the armour of Sir James and his knights, and mount their white horses. With Sir James gagged and dressed in Fulk's armour, his face obscured by the helmet, they ride off to see the King. When he sees them, he thinks that they are Sir James and his men bringing back Fulk as a prisoner.

When Fulk hands over his captive, the King orders the earl of Chester to kiss him. But Fulk says that he is so eager to hunt down the other FitzWarins, he does not have enough time to take off his helmet. The King then dismounts and gives Fulk his own fresh horse so he can pursue his enemies more quickly. Fulk then rides off.

The King orders that the captive be hanged. Sir Emery de Pyn, a Gascon and a relative of Sir James, volunteers to hang him himself. But when he takes off his helmet, he discovers that the prisoner is not Fulk. The King is furious and swears he will keep his armour on until he has taken Fulk and the other traitors.

Fulk and his men stop in a thicket after some six leagues (18 miles) to tend the injured. His brother William has been severely wounded and it is feared that he is going to die. The King soon catches up with them. When they see him coming, William begs Fulk to cut off his head and take it with him, so the King will not be able to identify his body. Fulk refuses.

The earl of Chester was to lead the attack. But, when he sees the FitzWarins, he halts his men and goes on alone to beg Fulk to surrender to the King. Fulk replies that he would not surrender for all the gold on Earth and begs a favour.

'My dear cousin,' he says, 'for the love of God I beg your help for my brother lying here near death. Promise me that after he dies you will make sure his body is buried so wild animals do not devour it. Please do the same for the rest of us when we are dead. Now, go back to your lord the King and do his bidding without hesitation or regard for us who are related to you by blood.'

When the earl resumes the attack, most of his men are killed as Fulk and his brothers defend themselves tenaciously. Fulk himself is injured when Sir Berard de Blois rides up behind him and slashes his side with his sword. Fulk turns, holding his sword in both hands. He hits Berard on the left shoulder. The force of the blow slices through his heart and lungs, and Sir Berard falls dead from his horse.

By then Fulk has lost so much blood that his sword falls from his hand and he slumps down on the neck of his horse. His brother John leaps up behind Fulk and they ride off. The rest then take to flight, pursued by the King and his men. They ride on all that night. In the morning they reach the place on the coast where Mador has their ship. Fulk is carried on board and John de Rampaigne tends his wounds.

When the earl of Chester finds William FitzWarin, he has him taken to a nearby abbey to be nursed. However, William is discovered there and the King has him carried on a litter to Windsor Castle, where he is thrown in a dungeon.

After seven days at sea, Fulk's ship reaches a rocky island called Beteloye off the coast of Spain. While the others go off to explore the small island, Fulk remains alone asleep on the ship. Suddenly, a storm blows up. The wind rips the ship from its moorings and it is carried out to sea. When Fulk awakes, he found himself alone.

The King of the Barbary coast, Messobrin, is standing on a tower in Tunis overlooking the sea when he sees a ship approaching. He sends two soldiers, who board the ship. Finding nothing except one knight asleep, they kick him and order him to wake up. Fulk jumps up and punches one of the soldiers, who falls overboard into the sea. The other flees. Messobrin then sends 100 knights to take the ship. Fulk defends himself bravely but he is forced to surrender. But, when he is taken to the palace, Fulk is given one of the royal chambers and waited upon.

The King's beautiful sister Isorie comes to visit Fulk and attend to the wound in his side. To bring solace to the handsome knight, she picks up a harp and starts singing. There is a commotion in the great hall. Fulk asks what is happening. Isorie tells him that messengers have arrived from Ydoyne, the beautiful daughter of the Duke of Cartagena. Long before, a dragon had carried her off to a high mountain and kept her there for over seven years, until a knight from England named Fulk, the son of Waryn de Metz, had killed the dragon and returned Ydoyne to her father. Soon after the duke had died and Ydoyne took over the duchy. The King of Barbary offered to marry her, but she refused him. Shamed by the refusal, Messobrin assembled an army and invaded Cartagena. Ydoyne fled abroad to raise troops. She has now returned with an army. However, she has sent messengers saying that, to save bloodshed, the battle should be fought between two champions. If her champion loses, she will give up her duchy and marry Messobrin. If he wins, Messobrin will return all the land he has taken.

Isorie then asks Fulk to be Messobrin's champion. Fulk refuses, saying he could never fight for a Saracen against a Christian. However, if the King will be baptized and become a Christian, he will be his champion. Isorie runs to tell her brother, who accepts.

On the day of the battle, Fulk faces Ydoyne's champion. Both knights spur their horses and exchange lance blows until splinters fly all over the field. Then they draw their swords. Fulk strikes his opponent's horse and it falls dead. When the knight hits the ground, he shouts: 'Wicked heathen, evil Saracen of pagan faith, may the God of Heaven curse you. Why have you killed my horse?'

Fulk dismounts and the two knights fight on foot well into the evening.

Finally the knight says: 'You, sir, may be a pagan, yet you are strong and noble. Please tell me where you were born.'

'I will not tell you until you tell me first,' says Fulk. 'Only then will I answer your question.'

The knight says that he was a Christian born in England. His name is Philip the Red. He had been stranded with his brothers on the island of Beteloye for more than half a year when the duchess arrived on a ship and rescued them. Immediately Ydoyne saw them, she had recognized them. She had been returning from England, where she had gone in search of the FitzWarins to help her in her war against the King of Barbary.

At that point Fulk interrupted:

'Dear brother, Philip the Red,' he says. 'Do not you know me? I am your brother Fulk.'

'You, sir, are a Saracen; you cannot be my brother,' says Philip.

Then Fulk shows him a secret sign, which Philip recognizes at once. The battle is adjourned. Philip explains to the duchess that it is his brother Fulk he has been fighting. Then Fulk and Philip take counsel with Messobrin. He and his household are baptized, and the King marries the duchess.

The King gives Fulk and his brothers gold, silver, horses, arms and many luxuries, filling their ship with riches, and they set sail back to England. Arriving there secretly, Fulk sends John de Rampaigne to find out whether his brother William is alive. John disguises himself as rich merchant and goes to London, where he is invited to stay by the mayor. Hearing that the wealthy merchants have brought rich cloths, jewels, horses and other valuables from foreign lands, the mayor grants permission for the merchant's men to land in England. At court, John sees a tall man with a long black beard and raged clothes, guarded by two men-at-arms, and is told that this is Sir William FitzWarin.

John de Rampaigne allays suspicion by plying the King and his courtiers with gifts. They have to be carried to court by his sailors, Fulk's men. They grab Sir William FitzWarin and carry him towards their ship, which is now moored near the palace. Then they head out to sea.

Fulk and his men stay in Brittany for six months, then return to England. This time they head for the New Forest where the King is hunting wild boar. Fulk and his men capture him, along with six of his knights, and take them back to the ship. There the King is forced to restore all their inheritances. As a token of good faith, he leaves his six knights as hostages until a truce could be proclaimed throughout England. This time, the King is as good as his word. Fulk and his men are pardoned and their possessions are restored.

Fulk then joins the earl of Chester in an expedition to Ireland, where he kills a giant. Then he retires to Whittington with his wife Matilda and their children. He distributes his treasures and lands among his servants and friends. In later life, Fulk realizes that he has sinned against God by killing many men, so he founds a priory at Alberbury in Shropshire. Shortly afterwards, Fulk's wife dies and is buried in the priory. Later Fulk marries another noble woman, Dame Clarice d'Auberville, who also gives him healthy children. His daughter Eve marries his friend Llewelyn the Great, Prince of Wales, after the death of his first wife, Joan.

One night Fulk is in bed when a bright light appears and he hears a thundering voice, saying: 'God has granted to you, His vassal, a penance which is of greater worth to you here than elsewhere.'

The bright light vanishes, but it leaves Fulk blind for the rest of his life. The *Fouke le Fitz Waryn* then concludes with Merlin involving Fulk in the tale of King Arthur and the Holy Grail.

There are numerous parallels between *Fouke le Fitz Waryn* and the tales of Robin Hood. But the records show that Fulk FitzWarin was a real person who actually existed – even though the poem has him pitted against dragons, rescuing damsels in distress and converting Muslims to Christianity at the drop of a hat. Robin's adventures are altogether more believable. Nothing fabulous happens. It could be that Fulk's existence was recorded because he was a noblemen, while Robin was a mere yeoman whose life was considered to be of little consequence. Certainly Robin of Locksley, the disposed earl of Huntington, bears a closer similarity to Fulk FitzWarin than he does to the Robin Hood of the ballads.

7

EUSTACE THE MONK

Another medieval romance that mirrors both *Fouke le Fitz Waryn* and the tales of Robin Hood is that of Eustache Busket, alias Eustace the Monk (1170–1217). Like Fulk FitzWarin, Eustache was a real person born in the Courset district of Boulogne. According to his biography, he studied black magic in Toledo, returning home to become a Benedictine monk at St Samer Abbey near Calais. He left the monastery to avenge his murdered father. By 1202 Eustace was steward to the count of Boulogne, Renaud de Dammartin, but around 1204 the two men quarrelled. Eustace fled and became an outlaw. Hiding out in the forest, Eustace duped and humiliated Renaud in a series of daring escapades, appearing before him in numerous disguises, ambushing him and his men, and time and again making off with his horses.

Eustace later became a pirate, establishing himself in the Channel Islands. From there, he preyed on ships in the Channel. In 1205, King John employed him in his struggle against Philip II of France. With a fleet of 30 ships, he raided the Normandy coast. But, in 1212, Renaud de Dammartin became John's ally, turning the King against him. Eustace changed sides, raiding Folkestone and other coastal villages. When civil war broke out in England in 1215, Eustace supported the rebel barons and ferried Philip's son, Prince Louis, across the Channel to make his bid for the throne. The following year, he was bringing reinforcements when he was met by an English fleet off Sandwich. On 24 August 1217, his flagship was surrounded. He was captured hiding in the bilges and was executed on deck.

Between 1223 and 1284, the life of Eustace the Monk was recorded by an unknown poet from Picardy in a work known as *Li romans de Witasse le Moine*. However, to the bare facts of Eustace's life, the poet has added fantastic exploits and adventures – just as the author of *Fouke le Fitz Waryn* had done. According to the poem, on his way back from Toledo, Eustace and his companions get into a fight in a tavern at Monferrant. He casts a magic spell that makes the tavern-keeper and her customers strip off their clothes. They straddle the wine casks and engage in a bawdy feast. Next, Eustace casts a spell on a cart-driver, making the horse and cart go backwards.

After he arrives at the monastery, Eustace causes havoc by casting more spells. The monks fast when they should eat. They go barefoot when they should wear shoes, and they swear when they should remain silent. He terrifies the cook by turning a side of bacon into an ugly old woman. And, in a tavern, he gambles away the monastery's books, statues and crucifixes.

Hearing of his father's death, Eustace leaves the monastery to seek justice from Renaud de Dammartin, Count of Boulogne. To settle the dispute, a judicial duel is arranged, but Eustace's champion is killed. However, the Count appoints Eustace as his seneschal, or steward, to look after his estate while he is away with Philip II, claiming the territories held by King John in France. However, Hainfrois, knight of Hersinguehans – the man accused of killing Eustace's father – turns the Count against him. Eustace is summoned to give an account of himself but, fearing a plot, he flees.

The Count seizes all of Eustace's possessions and burns his fields. Eustace the Monk swears revenge. Outside Boulogne, there are two mills, which Eustace sets fire to. He sends the miller into the city to tell the Count that he has lit two candles so that, at the feast he is hosting, his guest can see what they are eating. Hearing this the Count sounds a bell, outlawing Eustace, who seeks refuge in the forest of Hardelot that then surrounded Boulogne.

The Count pursues Eustace into the forest, where Eustace has posted two trusted watchmen, young men who he has raised since childhood. But one of them offers to lead the Count to Eustace in exchange for being made a gentleman of the court. The other watchman overhears the conversation and reports back to Eustace. When the first watchman arrives at Eustace's camp, Eustace asks him to cut a strip of willow and twist it into a cord. Then he puts it around the watchman's neck and pulls it tight. The watchmen admits betraying Eustace and asks to be allowed to make his confession before he dies. Eustace says there is no time for that as the Count is on his way, but he will hang him from a high branch so that he will he closer to God. Eustace then makes the man climb the tree and hangs him with the cord he himself had made.

Eustace mounts his horse and makes off before the Count arrives to find the hanged informant. The Count chases after Eustace, but cannot catch him. Instead, he manages to capture two of Eustace's sergeants and, in a fit of pique, has their eyes put out. Eustace again swears revenge. In retaliation, he maims four of the Count's men by cutting off their feet.

One day, Eustace disguises himself as a pilgrim and goes to see the Count. He tells him that he had been on his way from Bruges when he was robbed by a man who looked too like a monk to be one and asks the Count for justice as this false monk was nearby – and here he was telling the truth.

'What does the man look like?' asked the Count. 'Is he black or white, tall or short?'

'About my height,' said Eustace.

Then Eustace leads the Count and seven of his knights out to the spot in the forest where he said he had seen the monk. There they are surrounded by 30 of Eustace's men.

'Don't be scared,' said Eustace. 'I seek only reconciliation.'

The Count says that their differences can never be reconciled.

'Go then,' said Eustace. 'You came here in my safe-conduct, and no harm will come to you.' And they part company.

On another occasion, Eustace is wandering through the forest and meets a merchant from Boulogne who is on his way home from Bruges.

'How much money do you have?' said Eustace.

'Sir, I tell you truthfully, I have 40 pounds in a belt and 15 sous in my purse,' said the merchant.

Eustace takes it from him and leads the man into a thicket where he counts the money. Immediately he gives it back to the merchant.

'Go and may God be with you,' he said. 'If you had in any way lied to me you would have left here without a cent.'

The merchant thanks him for his generosity.

One day, Hainfrois of Hersinguehans goes into the forest to relieve himself when he stumbles across Eustace's camp.

'Dismount and join us for a meal,' says Eustace.

Fearing for his life, Hainfrois dismounts and, after the meal is over, he pleads for mercy.

'You killed my father and my cousin,' says Eustace, 'not to mention the mess you have gotten me into with Count Renaud. I would not seek reconciliation with him for the whole of France. But it is not the same between you and me. You and I have eaten together, so from this day forth you will have nothing to fear from me.'

Then he lets Hainfrois go. The knight goes directly to the Count to tell him what has happened. The Count then orders him to retrace his tracks. In the forest, they find Eustace disguised as a leper, carrying a begging bowl, a crutch and a wooden rattle. As soon as Eustace sees the Count approaching he begins to shake the rattle and the Count and his knights put 28 deniers into the bowl.

As the troop passes by, Eustace trips the last horse, knocks the rider out of his saddle and rides away. When the horseless rider tells the Count the leper stole his horse, the Count curses: 'By bowels, belly and legs . . . the damn monk has tricked us once again.' And the pursuit continues.

When Eustace spots the Abbot of Jumièges coming down the road, he stops him and asks him what he is carrying.

'What's it to you?' the Abbot replies.

This makes Eustace angry. He threatens the Abbot and forces him to get down from his horse. Then he asks how much money he has. The Abbot says that he has only 4 marks in silver. Eustace searches him and finds he has 30 marks. He gives the Abbot back 4 marks – the amount he claimed to be carrying – and keeps the rest.

One day when the Count is out hunting, a spy comes to tell him that Eustace is in the forest nearby. The Count then camouflages himself in his heavy brown cloak and sets up an ambush with his men. But one of Eustace's watchmen sees them and warns Eustace. A charcoal burner is passing, carrying his charcoal to market on a donkey. Eustace changes clothes with the man and smears coal dust on his face and hands. When Eustace approaches the ambush, the Count and his men do not recognize him, so Eustace shouts to them: 'My lords, what are you doing there?'

The Count replies: 'What's it to you, you scurvy fellow?'

Eustace says that he is looking for the Count of Boulogne to complain that he had been robbed by Eustace the Monk.

'Is he nearby?' asked the Count.

'In this very forest,' says Eustace. 'Go straight down this road if you want to talk to him.'

The Count and his men go down the road, find the charcoal burner dressed in the Monk's clothes and beat him.

'My lords,' says the charcoal burner, 'why are you beating me so? I have no money. These are the clothes of Eustace the Monk who at this moment is on his way toward Boulogne with my coal and my donkey. His hands and face are blackened with coal dust.'

The Count then sets off after Eustace. By that time Eustace has washed his face. He meets a potter and swaps the charcoal burner's donkey for the man's pots. Returning the Count asks Eustace, now disguised as a potter, if he has seen a charcoal burner.

'Yes,' says Eustace the Monk, 'he went down this road straight toward Boulogne, leading his donkey loaded with coal sacks.'

The Count and his men race after him. When they catch up with him, they beat him, tie him hand and foot, and lay him across the back of a horse. The potter screams and cries: 'My Lords, in God's name, have pity on me. Why are you doing this to me? I have done you no ill.'

'You scoundrel,' says the Count, 'you thought you could escape? I will soon have you hanged.'

But then one of the Count's knights recognizes the potter who he knew well.

'What devils have turned you into a coal-man?' says the knight. 'You used to be a potter; no man will ever stay healthy who takes on so many different trades.'

'My Lord, have mercy,' says the man. 'I gave my pots to the coal-man in exchange for this donkey and this coal.

May God strike him down. He rode off into the woods, shouting: "Pots for sale! Pots for sale!"'

The knight speaks to the Count, saying: 'Eustace is a shameful fellow! Just a short while ago he was dressed as a coal-man, now he has become a potter.'

'Quick, after the man,' says the Count. 'Bring to me everyone you meet today and tomorrow. I'll never catch the Monk unless I take all of them.'

By this time Eustace has gotten rid of all his pots, throwing them into a swamp.

When the Count goes to Neuchatel to set up court, Eustace follows him, dressed as a woman. His face is covered with a veil and he is sitting, spinning when a sergeant comes by, riding one of the Count's horses and leading another.

'Let me mount your horse,' says Eustace, 'and I will let you fuck me.'

The sergeant eagerly agrees.

'Climb up,' he says, 'and I'll give you four-pence if you let me fuck you. I will also teach you ass-play.'

'I declare, never has any man screwed thus,' says Eustace, lifting a leg to the horseman letting off a loud fart.

'Damsel, you farted!' says the sergeant.

'You are mistaken, sweet handsome friend,' says Eustace. 'That was the sound of the saddle cracking.'

They ride off into the forest side by side. After going a short way, the sergeant says: 'Let's not go any farther. I am riding my master's horse, and you have his best palfrey. We should conclude our business quickly.'

'Sergeant,' says Eustace, 'I too want to fuck, so let's get to our ass-playing quickly. Come closer.'

'Damsel,' says the sergeant, 'be careful there is no

trickery. If there is, I swear by Saint Mary's bowels I will kill you.'

'My lodge is just ahead,' says Eustace. 'Just a bit further now.'

A little further down the road, they bump into Eustace's men. Eustace grabs the sergeant by the scruff of the neck, saying: 'Get down off that good horse. You won't ride it any further. The palfrey too will stay here quite well. The Count will never mount it again.'

He leads the sergeant to a mud-pit then says: 'Sergeant, strip off all your clothes. I know how anxious you are to have a fuck.'

Once the sergeant is in the mud-pit, Eustace says: 'Now, about that ass-play! You can fuck at your leisure. You thought you would fuck me. Aren't you ashamed for wanting to bugger a black monk?'

'May God have mercy, do not put me to such shame here, sire,' says the sergeant. 'By Our Lady, I thought you were a woman.'

Eustace takes pity on the sergeant and lets him go after getting him to promise that he will tell the Count how he has been tricked. But the sergeant is too ashamed and leaves the country, never to return.

Li romans de Witasse le Moine also covers Eustace's service for the King of France, seizing important Channel ports and ferrying Prince Louis to England. But then in 1213, when the King loses his ships, Eustace is blamed for betraying the fleet. Eustace refutes the accusation, saying that no man is bold enough to furnish proof of such treason. And nobody does. So Eustace sets out to sea again with a great fleet of ships but soon he finds more than twenty English ships bearing down on him. The enemy sets out in skiffs and attacks his ships with long bows and crossbows. Eustace's men defend themselves nobly. Eustace wields an oar, killing many Englishmen, breaking arms and legs, and knocking others overboard. The English then attack from all sides with battle axes. Eustace's men manage to hold off the first wave. But then the English start hurling pots of finely ground lime on board. The wind kicks up great clouds of dust that gets into the Frenchmen's eyes and there is nothing they can do to defend themselves. The English board Eustace's ship, badly maul his men and take the nobles prisoner. Eustace is killed and his head cut off, ending the battle. The poem ends with the moralizing line: 'No man can live long who spends his days doing ill.' So perhaps Eustace was no Robin Hood.

Like Robin, Eustace, Fulk and Hereward the Wake demonstrated a great prowess with arms. Although occasionally outnumbered or undermined by treachery, they use their wits to escape, usually thanks to the stupidity of their enemies. All four men are masters of disguise. Like Robin, Eustace disguised himself as a potter – and a monk, a charcoal-burner, an inn-keeper and a prostitute. Fulk was also disguised as a charcoal-burner when he lured King John into the forest, promising to show him a fine stag. Once the King promises to restore Fulk's estates he is allowed to go. Eustace lures the count of Boulogne into the woods, again releasing him unharmed. Again Robin Hood uses the same tactics.

Fulk forces the King's merchants he has captured to dine with him before fleecing them. Eustace is also discriminating in who he robs. The merchant from Boulogne who admits he had 40 livres 5 sous was sent on his way unmolested. But when the Abbot of Jumièges says he had just 4 marks and Eustace finds his purse contains over 30, he returns four to the abbot and retains the rest. These are, again, tales told about Robin Hood.

8

REBELS

Later versions of the tale of Robin Hood set him clearly on the side of the solid Anglo-Saxon yeomen who are oppressed by the wicked Normans and parallels have been draw between Robin and Hereward the Wake, the leader of the last-ditch Saxon attempt to resist the Norman invasion on the Isle of Ely in 1070–71. Antagonism between the Saxon peasantry and the Norman gentry is a key element in the tale of Robin Hood. However, the Norman conquest had been completed more than a century before the earliest appearance of Robin Hood and, puzzlingly, Robin and his Merry Men are fiercely loyal to King Richard, a Norman who spoke no English and spent less than six months in the country. Indeed, he used England merely as a cash cow to fund his overseas adventures.

Hereward the Wake's origins are obscure. It has even been suggested that he was the son of Leofric, earl of Mercia, and his wife Lady Godiva, who famously rode naked through Coventry as part of a campaign to get her husband to lower taxes. According to the *Anglo-Saxon Chronicle* and the *Domesday Book*, Hereward was a small-time squire in south Lincolnshire who held lands from the abbeys of Crowland and Peterborough. It is thought that he had already turned outlaw before the Norman conquest, rebelling against Edward the Confessor (1042–66), whose court was more Norman than English in speech, habit and custom.

After William the Conqueror's victory at the Battle of Hastings in 1066, the Normans began to colonize England. However, there was considerable resistance. In 1070, Sweyn II of Denmark (1047–74) arrived at the mouth of the Humber and was expected to make a bid for the crown. He sent soldiers to secure the Isle of Ely as a base for an invasion. At that period it could be reached by sea-going vessels from the Wash and the River Ouse, while being protected to the landward side by swamps and waterways. The Danes were joined by local people, many of whom were of Danish extraction. Hereward's followers and a band of Danish sailors seized the opportunity to sack Peterborough Abbey to keep its treasures out of the hands of the newly appointed Norman abbot and took refuge on Ely. Soon after Sweyn made peace with William and the Danes returned home. Ely then became home to Anglo-Saxon fugitives, including the earl of Northumbria.

In 1071, William besieged the isle, taking it by building a causeway across the marshes. Hereward escaped, but it is not known what happened to him after that. It is thought that, like other rebel leaders, he was later reconciled with the King. A man named Hereward held lands in Warwickshire at the time of William's death and the surname Hereward lived on in Ely through the thirteenth century.

The cognomen 'the Wake' – thought to signify 'the wakeful one' – was added later, appearing first in the fourteenth century. However, it may derive from his relationship with the manor of Bourne in Lincolnshire which, from the mid-twelfth century, belonged to the Wake family.

Hereward the Wake was soon celebrated in ballads which, no doubt, exaggerated his exploits. During the first quarter of the twelfth century, a monk in Ely Abbey wrote the *Gesta Herewardi*. The author claimed that he drew on first-hand accounts. Though by then, presumably, Hereward was dead, a number of his comrades in arms would still have been alive and, though elderly, capable of recalling their old campaigns. Many incidences that appear in the *Gesta Herewardi* later appear in the tales of Robin Hood.

According to the *Gesta*, Hereward is of noble descent, his father being Leofric of Bourne, nephew of Earl Ralph the Staller, and his mother Eadgyth, the great-great-niece of Duke Oslac. He is handsome with very blond hair and large grey eyes. His limbs are sturdy. He is agile, graceful, generous and courageous – in every way the 'perfect man'. However, he spares no one he thinks to be in any way a rival. This caused trouble. His father found that he has to defend his son almost every day against those who want to kill him. Eventually his father grows tired of this and drives his son out. Hereward responds by stealing from his father's estate and distributing the spoils among his followers. His father then goes to King Edward and gets him declared an outlaw. Hereward is just eighteen years old.

Banished from his home, Hereward embarks on a series of adventures. He slays a monstrous bear in Northumberland, a braggart in Cornwall who is the suitor for the hand of the princess and the leader of an invading army in Ireland. Then he returns to the Cornish princess, attending her wedding in disguise. He rescues the girl and marries her to an Irish prince. On his way home from Ireland, he is shipwrecked in Orkney, then again in Flanders where he fights for the Count of Flanders against the neighbouring Count of Guines. He woos and wins an enterprising girl named Turfrida, despite the violent opposition of another knight, fights in two campaigns against rebellious Frisian armies and wins two valuable horses.

Hereward returns to England to find that it has been subjugated by foreigners. At Bourne, no one recognizes him. The locals are grieving over the death of Hereward's younger brother who, in Hereward's absence, had inherited his father's estates. However, the King had sent men to seize the property. Hereward's brother defended their mother when the intruders abused her, and killed two Frenchmen. They cut off his head and set it up over the gate of the house.

That night, Hereward hears the men who had killed his brother and taken his estates celebrating. He puts on his coat of mail and his helmet, and picks up his sword. As he approaches his father's house, he sees his brother's head over the gate. He takes it down, kisses it and wraps it in a cloth. Then he goes in.

Inside he finds the revellers are drunk. Soldiers lie with

their heads in women's laps. In their midst is a jester playing the lute. His songs revile the English and he performs a rude imitation of English dancing. In payment the jester demands a trinket that had belonged to the parents of the lad they had killed the day before. One of the girls at the banquet then speaks up.

'There still survives a distinguished soldier by the name of Hereward, brother to the lad killed yesterday and well-known in our country,' she says. 'If he were here, none of these men would be left alive when the sun rises tomorrow.'

The lord of the household is indignant. He said he knows Hereward. He is a thief and a traitor.

'He would have suffered death on the gallows, if he hadn't ensured his safety by running away, not daring to stay in any land this side of the Alps!' he says.

The jester joins in the abuse of Hereward, singing a song to accompaniment of the lute.

Unable to tolerate this any longer, Hereward leaps out and runs him through with a single thrust of his sword. Then he turns to attack the other guests. Some are too drunk to get up. Others are unarmed. So Hereward is able to lay low fourteen of them, together with their lord, singlehandedly. That same night he sets their heads over the gate where his brother's head had been.

In the morning, the neighbours and those living round about are filled with astonishment at what Hereward has done. All the Frenchmen in the district are frightened. They abandon the lands assigned to them and flee, lest the same thing should happen to them. When the news spreads, Englishmen flock to Hereward, congratulating him on his return to his native land. Although he has taken possession of his father's inheritance, he realizes he cannot hold it when the King hears what he has done. So he takes 49 of the bravest men from his father's estate and his kinsfolk and arms them. For a few days they take vengeance on enemies in the neighbourhood who still remain on their manors.

As leader of a growing army of fugitives, condemned and disinherited men, Hereward realizes that he needs to be raised to the rank of knight to command the appropriate authority. With no Saxon King to dub him, Hereward goes to the abbot of Peterborough, a man named Brand, of very noble birth, who girds him with the sword and belt of knighthood in the English tradition. Then a monk from Ely named Wulfwine, who was a friend of Hereward's father, knights his comrades. Hereward wants his men to be knighted this way because he has heard that the French have ruled that if anyone were knighted by a monk, cleric or any ordained minister they were not the equal of a true knight. Hereward would prove them wrong and he has almost all those serving under him knighted by monks. This became the custom at Ely, which Hereward defends when King William has subjugated the rest of the country.

Hereward learns that Frederick, the brother of the old Earl William de Warenne, is boasting that he will personally take Hereward into the King's presence for punishment or cut off his head and set it up at a crossroads on the public highway. He also says he will mutilate or drive into exile all those who continue to support Hereward or render him assistance. Hereward then discovers that Frederick has arrived in Norfolk with a military force. One evening while Frederick is plotting Hereward's death, the outlaw arrives and slays him.

Hereward goes to Flanders to see his wife Turfrida, but promises to return to England within the year. He has not been in Flanders a fortnight before he is invited by a highly celebrated knight named Baldwin to join a campaign against the Viscount de Pynkenni. During the campaign Hereward is picked out for special admiration. Once, when his boldness has carried him too far among the enemy, they kill his horse beneath him, leaving him alone and on foot. He slays seven attackers who rush to seize him. Eventually he is surrounded by a wall of enemies on all sides, but seeing his spirit and courage, their leaders call them off. They say it was shameful for so many to be attacking a single man. Even if they eventually beat him, there would be no victory in one man being overcome by such a number. Indeed, it would be a slur on their reputation. Though he might die in the end, he would deserve esteem above everyone else. A comrade on horseback then comes to rescue Hereward. Back behind the lines, he praises the generosity of the enemy who have let him live even though he has killed seven of their men. This event results in such goodwill on both sides that the warring parties are reconciled and they honour Hereward with gifts.

Hereward returns to England with his wife and his chaplain, Hugo the Breton, who, as well as being a priest, is a trained man-at-arms. At Bourne, he finds the manor entirely undisturbed as if no one dare enter it. Some of his men are in hiding, but quickly rally to him. Others are scattered throughout the kingdom. When he left, he had arranged a signal for them – he was to set fire to three villages on Brunneswold near to Bourne. After they are in flames, he retires into the forest and waits for his men to gather around him.

The men who assemble are not considered to be of knightly rank unless first they achieve some notable deeds. Among them is Wulfric the Black, who got his name because he had once daubed his face with charcoal and gone unrecognized into a garrison and killed ten of the enemy with a single spear. Then there is his friend Wulfric Rahere, who rescued four brothers who were entirely innocent from a hangmen – the sort of thing Little John might do.

When the people on the Isle of Ely hear that Hereward has returned to England, they invite him to join them in the defence of the homeland and their fathers' liberties. The message is delivered in the name of Thurstan, abbot of the church at Ely, where the monks fear that a foreign prior will be set over them. Monks have already been sent from France, but a seaman named Brunman intercepted them at sea, ducked them in the ocean in a large sack that he tied to the prow of his ship, and carried them back to finance, saving the English monasteries from foreign domination for the time being.

Hereward accepts the invitation and boards a ship at Bardney in Lincolnshire. Hearing of this, the earl de Warenne, whose brother Hereward had slain, prepares ambushes along the roads that lead out to the isle through the swamp. However, Hereward learns about this when some of the earl's men are captured. They also tell him that the earl de Warenne himself will be lying in wait at Earith in Cambridgeshire the following day. Hereward skirts the ambush with his ships. Then he conceals his troops on the far river bank. Hereward with three knights and four archers rides forward to the river bank where the earl de Warenne's men can see them. They do not recognize Hereward and offer his men money and honours if they will betray him. In response, Hereward's men abuse and threaten the earl de Warenne's men, and tell them they should tell the earl that the man they are seeking is already on the far side of the river. When the earl hears this, he urges his men to swim the river to avenge his brother. They say that this is impossible; Hereward intends to trap them that way. All the earl can do is shout across the river: 'Oh, would that your master, that limb of Satan, were in my grasp now; he should truly taste punishment and death!'

Hereward replies: 'But if by good luck we two happened to be by ourselves anywhere, you wouldn't be so keen to have me in your feeble grasp nor be glad that we met!'

Then Hereward fires an arrow with such force, that although it rebounds from the earl's mail coat, it knocks him from his horse, rendering him unconscious. His men carry him away, while Hereward and his followers carry on to the Isle of Ely.

When the King hears about this he grows angry and decides to take the Isle by storm. He moves his whole army to Aldreth where the water surrounding Ely is narrower, just 4 furlongs (half a mile) wide. They bring timber and stone and begin building a causeway out through the swamp. At the river, they join large tree-trunks together with beams, supported underneath by inflated sheepskins. However, greedy for plunder, the whole army rushes on to the bridge all at once, the roadway sinks and the soldiers are all drowned, except for one man out of the entire company who reaches the Isle.

The monk who wrote the *Gesta* remarked: 'To this day many of them are dragged out of the depths of those waters in rotting armour. I've sometimes seen this myself.'

Seeing his men drown, the King gives up all hope of taking the Isle. However, the few men he has left are deployed as guards to prevent the islanders having free passage to the surrounding land.

The one man who reached the Isle is called Deda. Led before the dignitaries of the Isle of Ely, he is praised for his bravery. They ask him to stay for a few days so that he can see what a secure position they hold. Until then, Deda believed that the English knew little about war. But he says at Ely he can see that their strongly fortified location is occupied by courageous soldiers. Affirming that with an oath, he is given a gift and allowed to leave.

When Deda returns to court, he tells the King everything he has seen. Above all he praises Hereward and his men. They are better than any of the knights he has seen among the French, or in the German Empire, or at Byzantium. The earl de Warenne grows angry, saying that Deda has been deceived by Hereward. Deda's response is that he is only reporting what he has seen with his own eyes. The King asks whether the outlaws are well supplied. Deda says that the Isle is fertile. They have grain and domesticated animals, and there are fish in the surrounding waterways. When he stayed there, he says, he got sick from feasting and he urges the King to make peace with Hereward rather than waste the lives of more men.

Raiding parties are sent out to loot French possessions in the area, but those who came up against Hereward praise him for his courage and generosity to his enemies. The King wants to make peace with Hereward. His advisers are against it, but he protests that there is little he could do against Hereward as Ely was so easy to defend. Then a knight named Ivo de Taillebois speaks up.

'For a long time now I've known a certain old woman who could by her art alone, if she were present, crush all their courage and defence and drive them all out of the island in terror,' he says.

The King orders the hag to be brought to him secretly. In the meantime, the army surrounds the Isle. The inhabitants find themselves cut off, so Hereward decides to go out and reconnoitre disguised as a potter – just as Robin Hood would do later. He cuts his hair and beard and dons a greasy cloak. Then, with a consignment of pots, he makes his way to the King's court at Brandon. There he stays at the house where the witch was lodging. Imagining him to be an ignorant peasant who does not understand their language, the French speak openly about their plans to destroy those who are defending the Isle.

Early next morning Hereward visits the King's kitchens to sell his pots. One of the town bailiffs comes in by chance and remarks he has never seen a man so much like Hereward in his appearance and bearing – inasmuch as a poor man could resemble a man of noble birth. Hereward is then led into the King's hall so the knights and squires can see him. But they dismiss the resemblance, saying that a man of such moderate height could scarcely boast the bravery attributed to the Saxon knight. Others ask him if he knew the scoundrel Hereward.

'Would that I had that limb of Satan here among us now; then I'd get my own back!' replies Hereward. 'He's more detested by me than anybody, for he stole a cow of mine, four sheep, and everything I had, except for my pots and my nag, which up to now have been the livelihood of me and my two boys!'

Back in the kitchens, the kitchen staff get drunk. They begin making fun of the poor potter. They try to shave his head and pluck out his beard. Then they blindfold him and put his pots around him on the ground so he stumbles over them and breaks them. But when one of them hits him, he hits him back so hard that the man falls to the ground insensible. Seeing this, the other servants pick up pitchforks and attack Hereward. Grabbing a piece of wood from the fireplace, Hereward defends himself, killing one of his attackers and wounding others. Word spreads and Hereward is arrested. While one guard tries to load Hereward with shackles, his companion guards him with an unsheathed sword. Hereward grabs the sword and kills the man. He escapes, killing a page on the way.

While all this is taking place, the King is out hunting and the scene is reminiscent of Little John's fight with the Sheriff's kitchen staff while he, too, was out hunting.

With Hereward on his way back to Ely, one of his pursuers is deep in the forest when his horse unexpectedly succumbs to fatigue. Hereward comes across him by chance and asks who he is. The man replies: 'One of the servants from the King's retinue who have been pursuing a fugitive peasant who by guile today killed his guard and one of the King's pages. So if you've seen or heard anything, for God's sake, and of your kindness, tell me!'

'Well, since you ask for God's sake,' said Hereward, 'and appeal to my kindness, let me tell you that I am myself the man you're looking for.'

He takes the man's sword and lance, but lets him keep his life providing he promises to tell the King of their encounter. When he hears the tale, the King again praises Hereward as a generous and most remarkable knight. Nevertheless, he begins a new attempt to take Ely. He takes his entire army to Aldreth and orders all the fishermen in the area to bring their boats to Cottenham to ferry the materials needed to build fortifications.

Hereward shaves off his beard and hair, then disguises himself as a fisherman and comes with all the rest. All day they ferry timber across the river. That night, when they have finished work, Hereward sets fire to the timber. The fortification is burnt and several men are killed.

When it is learnt that Hereward has again escaped with impunity, the King declares that it is shameful to be ridiculed by him so frequently. However, he commands that Hereward should be brought to him alive. The Normans then guard the site at Aldreth more closely. After a week they have completed one platform and set up four wooden bastions to carry the siege-engines. Meanwhile the outlaws have built ramparts on the Isle opposite them.

Then the French army attacks with the witch in a raised position in their midst. Protected from all sides, she chants and casts spells. Then she bares her arse at them three times. But Hereward's men have made their way out through the swamps and set fire to reeds and brambles. The wind blows the smoke and flames towards the King's men who flee for their lives. Many lose their way and disappear into the swamp. Others are cut down by arrows. Knights find their lances useless against these guerrilla attacks. Even the King arrives back at camp with an arrow sticking from his shield. In the tumult, the witch topples from her elevated position, falls to the ground and breaks her neck.

Around this time the so-called 'Revolt of the Earls' takes place. Earl Ralph Guader secretly assembles a very large army. Then he invites many distinguished English people to his wedding and by force and trickery compels them to swear an oath binding themselves to him. He then takes over the area between Norwich, Thetford, and Sudbury. Thinking he is making a bid for the throne, the three earls and all those of high birth on Ely go to join him, leaving Hereward and his men to guard the Isle alone.

As the King has failed to take the Isle by force, he decrees that all the surrounding lands owned by the churchmen of Ely will be divided among his royal guard. The Abbot of Ely had gone to join the Earl of Guader at Bottisham, but when the revolt is put down he returns to the Isle. Hearing of the decree, he decides to make peace behind Hereward's back, providing the King returns the church land. The King agrees and arrangements are made for him to occupy the island while Hereward and his men are out foraging, to prevent further bloodshed. When Hereward hears of this, he goes with brands to set fire to the church and town, but is dissuaded by a monk. As the King is already at Witchford, he goes by boat to a large lake near Upwell where he waits for his men who have been out attacking Soham. Two of them disguise themselves as monks, tonsuring each other, as best they can, with their swords.

Hereward now finds himself under siege. He even kills his own prized horse, so that no lesser man can boast that he has taken it. Eventually, he and his men escape over Brunneswold and go into hiding in the great forests of Northamptonshire. The King then assembles an army from the counties of Northamptonshire, Cambridgeshire, Lincolnshire, Leicestershire, Huntingdon and Warwickshire. Hereward and his men elude them by putting the shoes on their horses back-to-front. But as the King's men close in from every side, it is clear that they are going to have to fight. He positions his archers and slingsmen in the branches of the trees, then Hereward and the rest of his men advance under their covering fire.

Despite being vastly outnumbered, the horsemen make repeated forays on to the enemy lines, breaking through and doing as much damage as possible before galloping back to the safety of the greenwood, where the Normans dare not follow them because of the men in the branches above. Late in the afternoon, the Norman knights grow tired and turn for home. Hereward attacks again, capturing many men, including five of some importance. One of them is the Abbot of Peterborough who is ransomed for £30,000. The Abbot then declares war on Hereward, giving church lands to knights who will help him. When Hereward hears of this, he rides to Peterborough, sets fire to the town, plunders all the treasures of the church and chases the abbot into hiding.

The following night in his sleep, Hereward sees an old man before him who warns that, if he wishes to avoid a miserable death the next day, he should return everything he has taken from the church. When Hereward awakes, he is seized by a sense of dread. Within an hour, everything he has stolen had been taken back.

Now a fugitive, Hereward continues his journey with his men. That night they get lost, but a wolf appears to guide them and lamps appear on the ends of their lances lighting the way.

Hereward has only been in Stamford for three days when he hears that a particular, unnamed, enemy is coming to get him. Hereward goes out to meet him. The man flees. Hereward pursues him from house to house. He follows him with an unsheathed sword and a small shield in his hand right into the great hall where many of the man's neighbours are feasting. With Hereward on his heels, the man flees into the interior of the house where, after putting his head through the hole in a lavatory seat, he begs for mercy. But in an astonishing act of mercy, Hereward does not touch him. Nor does he inflict any injury in word or deed. He simply returns the way he came, through the middle of the house, astonished that no one at the feast even wants to upbraid him. They have nothing in their hands but drinking-horns and wine-cups.

The widow of earl Dolfin, the most beautiful and wealthy woman in the realm, contacts Hereward, saying that she could get the King's permission for them to marry if he makes peace. Charmed by the beauty of the woman, Hereward gives his consent and sends his first wife Turfrida to Crowland to become a nun.

Hereward is on his way to court when he meets a tall Saxon soldier named Letold, who is renowned for his courage and skill in war. Hereward is courteous, but Letold is haughty and calls him a simpleton and peasant. Finally, they come to blows. Hereward's three companions overcome Letold's five men, but Hereward will not let them join in his fight with Letold, considering it shameful for two to fight against one. Unexpectedly, Hereward's sword breaks off at the hilt, then he stumbles over a helmet. One of his men offers to take his place in the fight, but Hereward draws another sword and continues. Feigning an attack on the head, he strikes Letold in the thigh. The soldier continues defended himself for some time on his knees, declaring that he will never surrender as long as there is life in him. Hereward praises his bravery and lets him go on his way. Later he praises Letold to his men, saying: 'I've never found such a man, nor did I ever meet with his equal in courage! Nor have I ever been in such danger when fighting anybody, nor had so much difficulty in conquering anyone.'

Hereward continues his journey to court with his three companions. But on the way he thinks that it will not be very impressive to turn up at court with so few men, so he returns with 40. But the King will not allow Hereward's men to stay along with his courtiers in case there is trouble. He gives instructions for them to be entertained at the next town. The following day, the King goes to inspect Hereward's soldiers and is very impressed. Hereward now expects the whole of his father's estate to be returned to him.

However, it rankles with some of the courtiers to see former enemies come into favour, so they urge an eminent soldier called Ogga to challenge Hereward in single combat – knowing that Hereward never refuses a challenge. They go out into the woods where they fight. But Hereward does little more than defend himself, saying that it is stupid to fight the whole day over nothing at all. Ogga takes this as a sign of weakness and continues attacking. Hereward thwarts his attacks over and over again. But, finally, unwillingly, he is forced to make a stand. He kills Ogga, though he is seriously wounded in the right arm in the process.

Others at court urge the King not to surround himself with traitors and blame Hereward for the fact that England has not been pacified. The King resists their arguments, but to placate them he puts Hereward in the custody of a respected man named Robert de Horepol. He is kept in fetters for a year in Bedford. After the year is up, the King is disposed to set him free, but the earl de Warenne and Ivo de Taillebois remain hostile and persuade the King that Hereward should continue to be held at the castle of Rockingham in Northamptonshire. While he is being transferred, the escort is ambushed by Hereward's men. Hereward begs them not to harm Robert de Horepol or his men. He then thanks Robert for his kindness and asks him to make representations on his behalf to the King.

Robert de Horepol goes to the King and tells him what has happened. The King concedes that he has treated Hereward unjustly. He immediately pardons him and returns all his father's lands. Hereward lives on for many years faithfully serving King William and his compatriots and friends. Just like the tale of Robin Hood, the *Gest Herewardi* ends with our hero being reconciled to the King, albeit a different one.

The fifteenth-century Scottish historian Walter Bower placed Robin Hood among the dispossessed followers of Simon de Montfort. French by birth and education, de Montfort came to England in 1229. With the help of his cousin Ranulf, earl of Chester, he became earl of Leicester and a favourite of Henry III. In 1238, Henry arranged for him to marry his sister Eleanor, even though she had previously taken a vow of chastity. When the barons protested, Henry turned against de Montfort and Eleanor, driving them from England. De Montfort went on a crusade with the King's brother Richard, duke of Cornwall. In 1242, he joined Henry's disastrous invasion of France, returning to the King's favour after covering Henry's escape following his defeat at Saintes. However, de Montfort was on the twelve-man committee appointed in 1244 to handle the growing crisis between the King and his barons. In 1248, he was sent to pacify Gascony, then an English possession. He crushed the revolt so ruthlessly that the Gascons complained to Henry and de Montfort was recalled to England to face charges. He was acquitted.

In 1254, Henry agreed to finance a papal war in Sicily, provided Pope Innocent IV (1243–54) put his infant son, Edmund, on the Sicilian throne. Four years later Pope Alexander IV (1254–1261) threatened to excommunicate Henry for not paying up. Henry appealed to the barons, but they only agreed to help if he acceded to their demands. In 1258, under the Provisions of Oxford, they created a fifteen-member privy council, selected by the barons, to advise the king and oversee the entire administration.

By this time, Simon de Montfort had become convinced that Henry was unfit to rule. He was opposed by the more conservative Richard de Clare, earl of Gloucester. When the King lent his support to Gloucester, civil war broke out. In May 1264 Simon de Montfort won a resounding victory at Lewes, capturing Henry and his eldest son Edward. Without the support of the barons, de Montfort established a military dictatorship, ruling in Henry's name. However, striving to find some way of instituting government by consent, he called a parliament – the French *parlement* (from *parler* to talk) was originally the highest court of justice – of representatives of the boroughs and shires. This is the basis of the modern British parliament.

In May 1265, Prince Edward escaped captivity and rallied the royalist forces. They defeated and killed de Montfort at the battle of Evesham in August 1265. By this time Henry was weak and senile. Edward took charge of the government, before ruling in his own right as Edward I (1272–1307).

Roger Godberd, one of de Montfort's captains who survived Evesham, fought on as a bandit or rebel in and around the Sherwood Forest area until his capture in 1272. Again, he may well have contributed to the tales that built up around Robin Hood.

A connection has also been made between Robin Hood and his Merry Men and William Wallace and his followers – both rebelled against an oppressive English King. In Wallace's case it was Edward I (1272–1307) who, in 1296, deposed the Scottish King John de Balliol and declared himself ruler of Scotland. In May 1297, Wallace and a band of some thirty men killed William Heselrig, the English sheriff of Lanark, and burned the town. He may have already been known to the authorities. A document dated 8 August 1296 records the conviction of one Matthew of York, a cleric, of a robbery in Perth on 14 June 'in the company of a thief, one William le Waleys'. Could Matthew of York be an early Friar Tuck? The link between the thief 'William le Waleys' and the Scottish nationalist William Wallace is somewhat tenuous, but English propaganda depicted Wallace as a thief and a brigand – a Robin Hood.

While other Scottish leaders sought peace, Wallace and his growing band of followers attacked the English garrisons between the Rivers Forth and Tay. On 11 September 1297, an English army under John de Warenne, earl of Surrey confronted him outside Stirling. Although Wallace's army was greatly outnumbered, the English had to cross a narrow bridge over the Forth to reach the Scottish positions. There, they were slaughtered. De Warenne's second-in-command, Hugh of Cressingham, was killed. His body was flayed and his skin cut into strips – one of which Wallace was said to have made into a sword belt. Wallace then captured Stirling castle and, in October, invaded northern England, ravaging Cumberland and Northumberland.

In December, Wallace returned to Scotland where he ruled in Balliol's name. The people only lent him grudging supports as he had yet to face Edward I – known as 'the hammer of the Scots' – who was away fighting in France. But for the time being Wallace imprisoned or executed all those who refused to obey him. Edward returned to England in March 1298 and invaded Scotland on 3 July, defeating Wallace at Falkirk three weeks later. Wallace fled, burning Stirling and its castle, both of which were restored by Edward. He resigned as 'guardian' of Scotland to be succeed by Sir John Comyn 'the Red' and Robert Bruce, also known as Robert the Bruce, later King Robert I of Scotland.

Wallace appears to have rejected an offer of clemency from Edward I, and Scottish noblemen tried to confiscate his lands. In November 1299, he went to France to ask Philippe IV for his support, but Edward had married Philippe's sister Margaret two months before and Philippe had Wallace arrested. He was going to hand him over to Edward, but Edward asked merely that Philippe keep Wallace in France. However, Philippe liked Wallace and, by 1303, he was back in Scotland, taking refuge with his men in the Forest of Selkirk. While Sir John Comyn defeated the English at Roslin, Wallace led another raid into Cumberland. But without support from the Pope or the French, who just been defeated by the Flemmings, the Scots were forced to sue for peace. Wallace was outlawed. He continued a guerrilla campaign, for which he had a particular gift.

With a substantial reward on his head, it was only a matter of time before he was taken.

On 5 August 1305, William Wallace was arrested near Glasgow. He was taken to London and tried at Westminster Hall. A laurel crown was placed on his head, to mock, it was said, his boast that one day he would wear a crown there. He was convicted of treason even though, as he maintained, he had never sworn fealty to Edward I. On 23 August 1305, he was hanged, disembowelled, beheaded and quartered. He quickly became a folk hero and, around 1477, Henry the Minstrel, commonly known as 'Blind Harry', wrote *The Actes and Deidis of the Illustre and Vallyeant Campioun Schir William Wallace*. Like many of the works of that period it has been criticized for its lack of historical accuracy. It is wildly romanticized and some of the episodes were plainly made up – such as a victory where he reverses the defeat at the battle of Falkirk and an invasion of England that he halts at the pleading of the English queen.

According to Blind Harry, Wallace entered a life of crime young, like Robin Hood – when, at the age of eighteen, he killed the son of Selby, the constable of Dundee. Harry presents the death of Heselrig as Wallace's revenge for the murder of his mistress, Marion Braidfute, who had spurned Heselrig's son. An eyewitness quoted in the *Scalacronica* – a Scottish chronicle written by Sir Thomas Gray of Heaton while imprisoned in Edinburgh after an ambush in 1355 – describes the death of Heselrig as the political assassination of a hated English official. Blind Harry also said that Wallace went to Aberdeen where he burnt a hundred English ships. If this incident occurred, it was more probably the work of Andrew Murray, who led the rebellion in the north.

Published in around 1508, Blind Harry's poem was one of the first books to be printed in Scotland. It went through twenty-three editions before the Act of Union united England and Scotland in 1707. In 1722, it was given new life when it was translated into contemporary English and adapted by another poet, William Hamilton of Gilbertfield. Rewritten in novel form in 1810 as *The Scottish Chiefs*, it became a bestseller, and was translated into Russian, German and French – though it was banned by Napoleon who considered it dangerously subversive. Then, in 1995, it became the basis of the Mel Gibson film *Braveheart*.

Down the centuries Robin Hood and his Merry Men have been associated with other resistance movements. Robin's name was coupled to the Peasants' Revolt of 1381. This occurred in the aftermath of the Black Death that struck England in 1348 and killed one-third to one-half of the population. With a shortage of agricultural labour, wages rose, but as there was less surplus produce prices also soared. Parliament passed legislation restraining wages, but prices were not similarly controlled. Meanwhile, the court of Richard II (1377–99) was notably extravagant and, to finance an expensive and unsuccessful war in France, a poll tax was introduced. At first it was set at 4 pence a head, but in 1381 it was raised to one shilling – 12 pence. The trouble began with attacks on tax collectors, but then the revolt became more widespread. Peasants attacked their feudal masters and destroyed the documents that assigned them villein – or serf – status. Lawyers who wrote these documents were also attacked, along with the religious houses that upheld the feudal system.

There was a general uprising across south-east England. The men of Essex and Kent marched towards London. Admitted to the city by sympathizers, they attacked Fleet prison and John of Gaunt's Savoy Palace. The fourteen-year-old Richard II rode out to meet the protestors at Mile End and made various promises. But, later that day, protestors broke into the Tower of London, then the seat of government, and killed the chancellor, the treasurer and other officials.

The next day the King met the rebels again at Smithfield. During the negotiation the peasants' leader Wat Tyler was attacked and killed by the mayor of London. His followers, who had exhausted their supplies, drifted home. Richard II then reneged on all the promises he had made, saying: 'Villeins ye are and villeins ye shall remain.'

The Peasants' Revolt has another connection with Robin Hood. It occurred during the Hundred Years War between England and France that stared around 1337 and ended in 1453. This was the period when the English archer reigned supreme. The English longbow – the weapon now most commonly associated with Robin Hood – seems to have been developed in Wales. It was as tall as a man with arrows half that length. A trained archer could fire six aimed shots a minute with an effective range of 200 yards – though it was possible to fire an arrow twice that distance.

The effectiveness of the English longbow was first demonstrated against the Scots at the Battle of Dupplin Moor in 1332 and Halidon Hill in 1333. Flemish crossbows proved no match at the Battle of Cadzand in 1337. And the French got their first a taste of them at Sluys in 1340. Nevertheless they seemed unprepared when the English King Edward III (1327–77) and his son, Prince Edward, later known as the Black Prince, landed at Cherbourg in July 1346.

They were heading for Rouen when they heard that Philip VI (1328–50) of France was massing an army near Paris. With the bridges across the Seine cut, Edward moved his army north to retreat into Flanders. But his way was blocked by the River Somme. With a massive French army on his tail, he eventually made a crossing near Blanchetaque. Then he turned to face the French outside the village of Crécy. It was there that 6,000 English archers – ordinary yeomen – with 2,000 in reserve, cut down the flower of French nobility.

Ten years later, in 1456, the French again sent heavily armed knights against English archers at Poiters. Philip VI's successor King John II – 'John the Good' (1359–64) – and his son Philip were captured, along with seventeen lords, thirteen counts, and five viscounts. In all, the French suffered 2,500 dead and wounded, and 2,000 captured. The Black Prince reported casualties of just 40 English dead.

At Agincourt in 1415, sturdy English archers again cut down French knights with arrows tipped with armour-piercing 'Bodkin points'. Then they dropped their bows and finished off the dismounted knights with swords and axes. In battle, the ordinary English yeoman showed that he was more than equal to any French noble and his fine charger. This fighting spirit suffuses the subtext of Robin Hood. The Merry Men – yeomen to a man – repeatedly take on French knights of Norman descent and beat them. After Agincourt, the English bowmen remained supreme until the Battle of Formigy in 1453, when they were overwhelmed with fire from French handguns and cannons. By then, the only English possession remaining in France was Calais, which was lost in 1558.

9

THE MERRY MEN

Little John

Little John was with Robin Hood from the start. Andrew Wyntoun mentions him alongside Robin in the *Original Chronicle* in 1420. Indeed, he put Little John first in the lines 'Litil Johun and Robert Hude, Waythmen war commendit gud', indicating, perhaps, that Little John was perhaps more important that Robin, leader of the gang. Or Wyntoun may simply have put Little John first so he could rhyme 'Hude' with 'gud'.

Walter Bower puts Robin and Little John – along with the 'accomplices from among the dispossessed' – together again in the *Scotichronicon* in the 1440s. Little John is with Robin in the early ballads, *Robin and the Monk* and *Robin and the Potter*. He is also a central character in *A*

Gest of Robyn Hode, and one of the 'seven score and three' men that Robin took to court after he had been pardoned by the King; after a year, he is one of the two left. But no mention is made of him when Robin returns to the green wood. Nor is he with Robin in Kirklees when he was betrayed and murdered by his cousin the Prioress and her lover Roger of Doncaster.

However, Little John does appear in *The Death of Robin Hood*. In it, Robin takes Little John with him to Kirklees. He is sitting under a tree when he hears Robin blowing weakly on the horn after being bled by the Prioress. Fearing Robin is dying he breaks into the building. They are escaping through a window when Robin sees off Red Roger, but he is mortally wounded in the process. Little John holds Robin's hand to give him the strength to make his Confession. Robin then denies Little John permission to set fire to the hall because, if a widow was hurt in the process, God 'would blame me'. He had never hurt a woman in his life and he did not want to be responsible for hurting one at his death. Then Robin asks for his bow and let an arrow fly. Robin tells Little John, where the arrow hits the ground, that's where his grave should be and gives his loyal friend detailed instructions about his burial, which were followed to the letter.

There is also a ballad called *Robin Hood and Little John*. It was found in a collection published in 1680–85, though, again, it is certainly much older. Plays called *Robin Hood and Little John* were registered in 1594 and 1640, though they may have been dramas drawn from *A Gest of Robyn Hode* or *Robin Hood and the Monk*. A ballad with the title *Robin Hood and Little John* was registered in 1624, which is almost certainly the same as the one published in the 1680s. It is thought to have been written by a professional ballad writer as a 'prequel' to the *Gest*, explaining how Robin met Little John and how he got his name.

It begins when Robin was twenty years old and was already living in the forest with his Merry Men. One day, he complained that he had not had any sport for a fortnight, said goodbye to his men and headed off on his own. On a narrow bridge over a brook, he met a stranger who was seven foot tall. Neither would give way, so Robin pulled an arrow from his quiver. The stranger said that he would tan Robin's hide if he pulled back his bow string. Robin replied that the stranger was prating like an ass. He could fire an arrow through the stranger's heart before he could strike one blow.

The stranger accused Robin of being a coward for threatening him with a bow and arrow when he was only carrying a staff. So Robin put down his bow and cut himself a staff. Then he got back on to the bridge and they started to fight. Robin had the first hit, causing the stranger's 'bones to ring'. Next the stranger struck Robin on the crown and blood began to flow. Robin grew angry and rained down blows on the stranger. This made the stranger angry too and he hit Robin one blow that sent him tumbling into the river.

> 'I prithee, good fellow, O where art thou now?'
> The stranger in laughter he cry'd
> Quoth bold Robin Hood, 'Good faith, in the flood,
> And floting along with the tide.'

Robin conceded defeat and the battle was at an end, but when he pulled himself out on to the bank he sounded a blast on his bugle-horn and his bowmen appeared.

'What's the matter?' said William Stutely, and asked Robin why he was soaked to the skin. Robin replied that, in their fight, the stranger had knocked him in.

The Merry Men seized the stranger to give him a ducking, but Robin stopped them. He asked the stranger to join his band, which then numbered 69, and wear his livery: the Merry Men's suit of Lincoln green. Robin also offered to teach him how to use a bow so that he could shoot fallow deer – this is odd as in earlier versions of the story, notably *Robin Hood and the Monk*, Little John was a better archer that Robin.

The stranger offered his hand and agreed. He said his name was John Little, but Will Stutely said his name would have to be changed and he would be his godfather.

Before the baptism, they put on a feast, which was hardly necessary. As well as being seven foot tall, John Little had a 45-inch waist. Amid much drinking, John Little was baptized Little John. Robin then clothed him head to foot in green and gave him a longbow. He told Little John that, in the forest, they lived like squires or lords of renown, although they owned no land. They lived off good cheer, wine and ale. And they would not be without gold or silver while they could empty bishop's purses. After music and dancing, the Merry Men retired to their caves. And from that day forward, though he was conspicuously large, John Little was called Little John.

In the *Gest of Robin Hode*, Little John is also known as Reynold Greenleaf. This is the same name Little John uses when he goes into service with the Sheriff in Howard Pyle's account of the story. However, elsewhere in the *Gest*, Reynold Greenleaf appears as a separate character and it is thought that the name might be a sobriquet applied to all outlaws. Indeed, Reynold Greenleaf could easily be rhyming slang for thief.

In the ballad *Little John a Begging*, which appeared in the mid-seventeenth century, Robin sends his men out begging, starting with Little John. This is a bit of a climb-down from Robin's earlier attitude of making a living by stealing from the rich, particularly wealthy clergymen. Little John does what he is told, though he insists on dressing as a palmer, an itinerant monk. He meets three beggars – one blind, one dumb and one crippled – rather as Robin did in Howard Pyle's version. Naturally, he gets in a fight with them and discovers that they are hiding hundreds of pounds in gold, which he takes back to Robin.

According to local tradition, Little John retired to the village of Hathersage in the Derbyshire Peak District. In the late seventeenth century, Elias Ashmole (1617–92) recorded:

> The famous Little John lies buried in Hathersage churchyard within three miles from Castleton in the High Peak, with one stone set up at his head, and another at his feet, but a large distance between them. They say that part of his bow hangs in the church chancel.

In the later eighteenth century, a grave was opened. The bones of a giant were said to have been found, including a thigh bone 29½ inches long. They were put on display in a window before they went missing. In 1929, the Ancient Order of Foresters renovated the grave. Again they marked it by two stones some thirteen feet apart and it bears the inscription: 'Here lies Little John, the friend and lieutenant of Robin Hood.'

In 1729, the bow was taken from the church to Cannon Hall near Barnsley. In 1951, the Stanhope family gave it to the Wakefield Museum. It has since disappeared.

The Derbyshire antiquarian James Myers discovered that a Jack Crawney owned a property in Hathersage in 1352. Searching the Wakefield Manor Rolls for the 1320s he discovered that a John Crawney was the blacksmith in the village of Woolley, where Elizabeth Staynton, who Hunter believes was the Prioress of Kirklees, came from. Myers believed that Jack Crawney and John Crawney were the same person. The last record of Crawney's name in Wakefield appears in 1322 so he might have been outlawed after the Lancastrian revolt.

Myers also claimed to have found letters dating from the eighteenth century in the collection of the Duke of Rutland whose ancestors owned the estate the village of Hathersage stood on. The letters, he said, referred to poems written in the fourteenth century by an elderly resident named Jack Crawley. From there he made the giant leap to the conclusion that *A Gest of Robyn Hode* was written by none other than Little John himself.

Court rolls show that in December 1318, there was a break-in at the house of Simon of Wakefield at Hornington and £138 was stolen. One of the gang involved was named 'John Le Litel'. Then in May 1323, William de Melton, Archbishop of York, recorded that a gang which included a man named 'Littel John' had stolen a deer from his park in Beverley, Yorkshire. The village of Holderness adjoins Beverley – in the *Gest*, Little John tells the Sheriff of Nottingham that he was born in Holderness.

Will Scarlet

Will Scarlet appears alongside Little John and Much the miller's son in the earliest ballads, *Robin and the Monk* and *A Gest of Robyn Hode*. His name is also rendered as Scathlok, Scatheloke, Scathelocke, Scarlett, Scarlock, Scadlock, Scarlok, Scalok, Scarelock, Scarllett, Scadlocke, Scardelocke, Shirlock or Skirlock. This led to some confusion and the Elizabethan playwright Anthony Munday featured Scarlet and Scathlock as brothers in *The Downfall of Robert, Earl of Huntington*. It is also thought that Will Stutely may also be another representation of Will Scarlet, rather than a separate character. It could have been that there were several men with similar names in Robin Hood's band, or that the name changed during the oral transmission of the ballads.

Originally, the word 'scarlet' did not refer to a colour at all. It meant 'a rich cloth, often of a bright red colour'. The word became associated with the colour because red dyes were rare and particularly expensive. Consequently, Will Scarlet is painted as a bit of a dandy. Early ballads and plays were often commissioned by guilds and, in those concerning Robin Hood, clothing and their colours are mentioned frequently, perhaps as an early form of advertising. Some of the earliest ballads say that Robin Hood wore red as well as green – perhaps a russet for winter camouflage in the forest. In one story he is said to have worn 'scarlet and green'. This many have been 'scarlet in grain', which is a 'shot-woven' red fabric with green on the cross-grain, producing a spectacular effect, especially in silk. But then the 'Lincoln green' that Robin's Merry Men traditionally wore may not have been green at all. Some authorities think that Lincoln green was in fact Lincoln graine, a shade of scarlet. Graine are the eggs of silk worms which, when crushed, give a bluish, purple dye.

On the other hand, etymologically, 'Scathlock' means 'lock-smasher', meaning a man so violent that he could not easily be locked up or imprisoned – a good name for an outlaw. The Chamberlain of Scotland made a payment to a William Schakelock in April 1305. There is another reference to a Schakelock who was a soldier in the Berwick town garrison in December 1316, and later a William Scarlet among the names of those who in November 1318 were granted pardons for felonies. Then again, a William Scathlock was a monk at St Mary's Abbey in York who was expelled in 1287. Nothing more is known of his life.

P. Valentine Harris searched the Wakefield manor court rolls for his book *The Truth About Robin Hood* and found an Adam Schakelock of Crigglestone, where Roger de Doncaster held land, listed in April 1317. Harris suggested that this could be a member of Will Scarlet's family.

The tale of Robin meeting Will Scarlet is told in the ballad *Robin Hood and Will Scarlet* – also known as *Robin and the Stranger* and *Robin Hood and the Newly Revived*. Robin sees a young man walking in the forest. He is dressed in a silk doublet, or a short tight-fitting padded jacket fashionable from the fourteenth to the seventeenth centuries, and scarlet hose or stockings.

There is a fight and Robin is wounded. Blood flows from a gash on his scalp. Robin then asks the stranger about himself. He says he comes from Maxfield and has been forced to take refuge with the outlaws in the wood after killing his father's steward. What's more he is seeking his uncle Robin Hood. Robin then takes his nephew in.

In this version of the tale Will Scarlet introduces himself as 'Young Gamwell'. This invites comparison with

The Tale of Gamelyn, another traditional poem from around 1350 that feeds into the tale of Robin Hood and the 'noble outlaw'.

The story takes place in the fenlands of Lincolnshire during the reign of King Edward I. The ageing Sir John of Boundes has three sons. The eldest, John, is a vicious and malignant character. The second brother, Otho, shows due reverence to their father, while the youngest, Gamelyn, is his father's pride and joy.

Instead of leaving all his estates to his eldest son, their father decides to divide them among the three boys. But when he dies, Gamelyn is still a minor, so John assumes control of his lands and lets them run to wrack and ruin. Gamelyn resents this. One day, when John asks him where his dinner was, Gamelyn objects to being treated like a servant and tells him to cook it himself.

'My dear brother, is that the way to answer?' says John. 'Thou hast never addressed me so before!'

'No,' says Gamelyn, 'until now I have never considered all the wrong you have done me. My parks are broken open, my deer are driven off; you have deprived me of my armour and my steeds; all that my father bequeathed to me is falling into ruin and decay. God's curse upon you, false brother!'

John calls his servants to beat Gamelyn. But Gamelyn leaps a wall, grabs a heavy pestle and fights them off. John flees to a loft and bars the door, but Gamelyn sees him peeping through a window.

'Brother, come a little nearer,' says Gamelyn, 'and I will teach you how to play with staff and buckler.'

John tries to make peace. He says that he will give Gamelyn everything their father had left him and even promises to repair the decayed mansions and restore the lands and farms to their former prosperity. They kiss and make up. Soon after, there is a wrestling match that Gamelyn is determined to win. John lends him a horse so that he can go to it and prays that he might break his neck while locking the castle gate behind him.

On the way to the wrestling match, Gamelyn meets a man whose two sons have been beaten by the wrestling champion and are not expected to live, but he is not put off. The match lasts into the late evening. Eventually, Gamelyn breaks the champion's arm and three ribs, and wins the match. But when he gets home to the castle with a crowd of supporters, the doors are barred against him. Gamelyn breaks down the door with one blow and flings the porter down the well. The other servants flee, while John takes refuge in a turret. Gamelyn then invites his supporters to feast with him and drink the five tuns of wine they would find in the cellar. The party went on for a week.

On the eighth day, when the guests have departed, John emerges from hiding.

'Who made thee so bold as to destroy all my household stores?' he asks.

'Nay, brother, be not wroth,' says Gamelyn quietly. 'If I have used anything I have paid for it fully before-hand. For these sixteen years you have had full use and profit of fifteen good ploughlands which my father left me; you have also the use and increase of all my cattle and horses; and now all this past profit I abandon to you, in return for the expense of this feast of mine.'

To placate Gamelyn, John says that, as he has no son of his own, he will make Gamelyn his heir. But he has a trick up his sleeve. After a moment's hesitation, he adds: 'There is one thing I must tell you, Gamelyn. When you threw my porter into the well I swore in my wrath that I would have you bound hand and foot. That is impossible now without your consent, and I must be forsworn unless you will let yourself be bound for a moment, as a mere form, just to save me from the sin of perjury.'

John seems sincere, so Gamelyn consents. He sits down so that the servants can bind him hand and foot. Once the ropes are secure, John says: 'So now, my fine brother, I have you caught at last.'

He gets the servants to fetter Gamelyn's arms and legs. Then they chain him fast to a post in the centre of the hall. Everyone who enters is told that Gamelyn has gone mad and has been chained up for his own safety. For two long days and nights he stands there bound, without food or drink. The fetters are so tight that he cannot sit or lie down and he grows weak from hunger and fatigue.

Eventually, Gamelyn is left alone with Adam Spencer, the elderly steward of the household and loyal servant of Gamelyn's father. Gamelyn asks Adam to release him. But this presents the old man with a dilemma. How can he reconcile his loyalty to his dead master with the loyalty due to his present lord, who he has now served for sixteen years. So Gamelyn promises him half of his lands if he would free him. When John is safely in bed, Adam gets the key and releases Gamelyn, then takes him to a private room and feeds him. As he eats and drinks, Gamelyn plots revenge.

'What is your advice, Adam?' asks Gamelyn. 'Shall I go to my brother and strike off his head?'

'No,' says Adam, 'I know a better plan than that. Sir John is to give a great feast on Sunday to many Churchmen and prelates; there will be present a great number of abbots and priors and other holy men. Stand as if bound by your post in the hall, and beseech them to release you. If they will be surety for you, your liberty will be gained with no blame to me; if they all refuse, you shall cast aside the unlocked chains, and you and I, with two good staves, can soon win your freedom.'

After mass that Sunday, guests thronged to the feast in the great hall where Gamelyn stands with his hands behind his back as if chained to the post. Food is brought, but none is given to Gamelyn, despite his pleading.

'Now I see that I have no friends,' he says. 'Cursed be he that ever does good to abbot or prior!'

Adam can see that Gamelyn is growing angry. He goes to the pantry and brings good oak staves. Then Gamelyn throws off his chains, seizes a staff and lays into the guests. The portly churchmen try to escape, while the laymen, who are on Gamelyn's side, draw aside to give him free play. He takes no pity on the clergy, who have shown no pity to him. He knocks them over, batters them, and breaks their arms and legs, while Adam warns him to shed no blood as spilling blood is sacrilege. Many have to be carried home on carts and wagons.

As in the tale of Robin Hood, vengeance is taken on rich priests.

Then Gamelyn turns his attention to his brother. He breaks his back with one blow from his staff and thrusts him into the fetters that still hung from the post where Gamelyn had stood.

'Sit there, brother, and cool thy blood,' says Gamelyn, while he and Adam tuck into the feast.

The sheriff happened to be just five miles away when news of the disturbance reached him. Gamelyn and Adam, he heard, had broken the King's peace and it was his duty to arrest the law-breakers. However, the new porter at the

castle was a supporter of Gamelyn. When the sheriff
arrives, he refuses him entrance and sends a servant to
warn his master. While the porter delays the sheriff at the
front gate, Gamelyn, Adam and their followers go out of
the back. Twenty-four of the sheriff's best men are waiting
for them, but they are quickly despatched with staffs.
Gamelyn's men are having a glass of wine in celebration,
when the sheriff himself turns up with more men.

'Let us stay no longer, but go to the greenwood,' says
Adam. 'There we shall at least be at liberty.'

After another glass of wine, they make off. Meanwhile,
the sheriff's men have entered the hall and found Sir John
fettered and near to death. They release him. Though
John is grievously wounded, he survives.

Gamelyn and Adam do not have a good time in the
greenwood. They find very little food there. Then one
day they hear men's voices nearby. Looking through the
bushes, they see seven score young men sitting round a
feast spread on the grass. Their leader sees the two of
them in the undergrowth and sends seven men to get
them.

'Yield and hand us your bows and arrows!' they say to
Gamelyn and Adam.

Gamelyn refuses.

'Why, with five more ye would be only twelve,' he says,
'and I could fight you all.'

When the outlaws see how boldly he carries himself
they change their tone.

'Come to our master,' they say, 'and tell him what you
desire.'

'Who is your master?' asks Gamelyn.

'He is the crowned king of the outlaws,' the men say
and lead Gamelyn and Adam to their chief.

The master-outlaw is sitting on a rustic throne with a crown of oak-leaves on his head. He asks them their business.

Gamelyn replies: 'He must needs walk in the wood who may not walk in the town. We are hungry and faint, and will only shoot the deer for food, for we are in a difficult situation and in great danger.'

The outlaw leader takes pity on them and gives them food. They eat ravenously. Meanwhile, the outlaws whisper one to another: 'This is Gamelyn!' They have heard of him and the evils that had befallen him. Knowing of his reputation, the outlaws' leader makes Gamelyn his second in command. Three weeks later the outlaw king is pardoned and allowed to return home. Gamelyn is chosen to succeed him and is crowned king of the outlaws.

After Gamelyn's brother John has recovered, he becomes sheriff and indicts his brother for a felony. When Gamelyn does not appear to answer the indictment, he is declared an outlaw, a fugitive to be hunted down and a price is put on his head. Hearing the bad news, Gamelyn goes to confront his brother. Alone, he strides into the great hall and demands to know why he has been declared an outlaw. But John has him arrested and thrown in prison.

For years, Otho has lived quietly on his own lands and stayed out of his brothers' feud. Now he is forced to act. He goes to John and begs him to show mercy for the sake of brotherhood and the family, but John insists that Gamelyn must stay in prison until the next assize. Otho offers to stand bail. John agrees to this, but warns Otho that he will suffer in his bother's stead if Gamelyn fails to appear before the court. Gamelyn is released on his brother's surety and goes back to the greenwood where he quickly falls back into his old ways, robbing fat abbots and priors, monks and canons. Nevertheless, he gains the reputation of being 'the courteous outlaw'. When the day of the trial approaches, he calls his men together and asks them to accompany him to the assize. Adam is sent ahead to find out what was happening. He returns with the news that the judge is already sitting and the jury has been empanelled. They have been bribed by John to condemn Gamelyn to death and Otho is in jail, in fetters, in the place of his brother. Adam is furious and says he would happily kill everyone in the hall, except Otho. But Gamelyn's sense of fair play prevails.

'Adam, we will slay the guilty and let the innocent escape,' he says.

While his men guard the doors of the hall, Gamelyn strides into the hall, appoints himself judge, and releases Otho, who has already been sentenced to hang.

'Brother, this day your enemies and mine will be hanged – the sheriff, the justice and the wicked jurors,' says Gamelyn.

Then Gamelyn berates the judge for polluting the waters of justice, condemning the innocent and fining the poor. He orders him to come down from the bench. When he does not, Gamelyn strikes him, cutting his cheek, and throws him over the bar, breaking his arm.

Gamelyn then sits on the bench, with Otho beside him. His brother the sheriff, the judge and the jurors are then put in the dock, charged with attempted murder. A jury picked from Gamelyn's men brings in a verdict of guilty. The prisoners are all condemned to hang. John, of course, tries to appeal to brotherly affection.

After their high-handed punishment of their enemies, Gamelyn and Otho go to lay their case before King

Edward, who, in the light of all the wrongs and injuries Gamelyn has suffered, pardons them. He appoints Otho sheriff and Gamelyn chief forester. His band of outlaws are also pardoned and given posts in the royal household. After a period in the greenwood, they have all been pardoned by the King, just like Robin Hood and his Merry Men.

Gamelyn and his brother settle down to a happy, peaceful life. Having no son, Otho makes Gamelyn his heir. Meanwhile, Gamelyn marries a beautiful lady and lives happily with her for the rest of his life.

There is another connection between *The Tale of Gamelyn* and the tale of Robin Hood. In occurs in a ballad, dated around 1450, called *Robyn and Gandelyn*. The name Gandelyn is assumed to be a corruption of Gamelyn, though there is some argument about whether the Robyn in this tale is Robin Hood as Robin was a common enough name. However, the ballad does find Robyn and Gandelyn out in the greenwood, hunting for deer. Robyn shoots one, but has only half finished skinning it when an arrow strikes him down and kills him. Gandelyn swears that he will not leave the greenwood until he has avenged the slaying of his master. He looks around and finds a little boy called 'Wrennok of Donne'. This harks back to the poem *Fouke le Fitz Waryn*, where one of Fulk's worst enemies is Moris Fitz-Roger. Moris's son was called Wrennoc.

Gandelyn and Wrennok then have an archery competition.

'What shall our mark be?' asks Gandelyn.

'Each other's heart,' said Wrennok.

Gandelyn gives Wrennok first shot. The arrow passes through the material of Gandelyn's breeches, but misses his thigh. Then it is Gandelyn's turn. His arrow pierces Wrennok's tunic and cleaves his heart in two. Now, says Gandelyn, you will never be able to boast they you killed both Robyn and his servant Gandelyn.

Will Scadlock has more unlikely adventures with Robin. In the seventeenth-century ballad *Robin Hood and the Prince of Aragon*, he is in the forest hunting deer with Robin Hood and Little John. They are feasting when a woman dressed in black arrives, riding a black horse. She tells them that the Prince of Aragon is besieging London, demanding the King's daughter as his wife. He will only give up his suit if champions can be found and defeat the prince and his two giants. She is one of four damsels who have been sent out into the country to find champions. The King has promised that whoever wins shall have the princess as his bride. The three men volunteer. Robin kills the prince, while Little John and Will Scadlock finish off the giants. The King then offers his daughter in marriage. But as she cannot marry all three of them, she is asked to choose. She choses Will. Then the earl of Maxfield steps forward. He is in tears, saying that Will looks like his dead son. Will falls to his knees and says that he is his son, still alive. Then Will and the princess marry.

Like Robin Hood and Little John, Will Scarlet has a grave. In the graveyard of the Church of St Mary in the village of Blidworth, Nottinghamshire, at the heart of old Sherwood Forest, there is an odd-shaped stone which is said to mark the grave of Will Scarlet. It stands between three yew trees, which are thought to symbolize death. According to local tradition, Will was killed by one of the Sheriff of Nottingham's men and was immediately avenged by Little John. In fact, the stone is the apex stone from the old church tower, which has ended up in the graveyard. Inside the church itself, though, there is a memorial to sixteenth-century Sherwood Forester Thomas Leake. Although he was not thought to have been a life-long outlaw, he often found himself at odds with authority and was eventually killed, so it is possible that he is the origin of the story that Scarlet is buried here. The village is also said to have been the home of Maid Marian.

Alan á Dale

Alan á Dale is a later-comer to the legend. He first appears as Allin á Dale – later spelt Allen, Allan and Alan – in the seventeenth-century ballad *Robin Hood and Allin á Dale*. The ballad tells the tale of Robin saving a young woman from an unsuitable marriage to an old knight and marrying her to her true love. This story was originally told about Will Scarlock in the Sloane *Life of Robin Hood* in the British Library. In *Robin Hood and Allin á Dale*, Robin originally sees 'a brave young man, as fine as fine might be' in the forest, who is dressed in 'scarlet red'. But the next day, he has cast the scarlet away. He is stopped by Little John and 'Nick the miller's son'. When he asks them what they want, they say they are going to take him to meet their master.

Robin asks him if he has any money. He replies that he has just five shillings and a ring, which he has kept seven long years for his wedding. He was to have been married the day before, but his love has been given to an old knight instead. Robin asks him what his name is.

'Allin á Dale,' says the young man.

Then Robin asks what 'gold or fee' he would give him to get his true love back. Allin says again that he has no money, but he would swear 'upon a book' to be Robin's true servant. Robin then hurries to the church where the wedding is to take place. The bishop, officiating, asks him what he is doing there. Robin says he is harp player, but refuses to play until he has seen the bride and groom. The groom, as Allin á Dale has said, is an old, though wealthy, knight, while the bride, 'a finikin [dainty] lass, did shine like glistering gold'.

'This is no fit match,' says Robin. 'The bride she shall chuse her own dear.'

He blows two or three blasts on his horn and 24 bowmen appear. As they march into the churchyard, they are led by Allin á Dale, who hands Robin his bow. Robin says that young Allin should now marry his true love. But the bishop says that the banns have to be read three times in church for the marriage to be legal. So Robin pulls off the bishop's gown and puts it on Little John. He then reads the banns seven times, in case three was not enough. Robin gives the bride away and they all return to the greenwood. Legend has it that the marriage took place in St James' Church in Papplewick, Nottinghamshire. Alan á Dale was also thought to have been buried there.

From this late ballad, Alan á Dale has become a staple in the modern rendition of the Robin Hood legend. He is usually portrayed as a minstrel – perhaps because Robin disguised himself as a harp player. As the original tales of Robin Hood come from ballads, it is also convenient to use Alan á Dale as the narrator of the story. Traditionally, in pantomime, while both Robin and Marian were played by men, Alan was played by a woman.

Much the miller's son

Alan á Dale has come to prominence at the expense of Much – or sometimes Moch, Moche, Nich, Nick or

Midge – the miller's son, who was one of the original Merry Men. In *Robin Hood and the Monk*, Much played a leading part and was one of the men who rescued Robin from prison. While Little John beheads the monk, Much despatches his page 'for fear lest he would tell'. Together they take the monk's letters and trick the King into giving them the royal seal to release Robin into their custody. Unlike Alan á Dale, Much is a seasoned fighter.

Much is also a leading figure in *A Gest of Robyn Hood* alongside Little John and Will Scarlok. Together they waylay the downcast knight. Much also appears in the play *George a Greene*, with Robin, Will Scarlet and Maid Marian, but not Little John who does not appear.

'Much' was not recorded as a Christian name, so it seems to have been a nickname. The play was set in Wakefield, where the mill stood on Wakefield Green. The family living there in 1322 were called Calder, though this was also the name of the river that turned the wheel. But there was nothing to link them to the earl of Lancaster's Contrariants.

Will Stutely

Will Stutely turns up in two ballads. In *Robin Hood and Little John*, he is the one who gives Little John his outlaw name. He gets his own ballad with *Robin Hood Rescuing Will Stutely*. In it, he kills two of the Sheriff's men and is arrested. When Robin hears the news, he vows to rescue Will. Robin dresses in scarlet, while his men remain in green. They set out for the castle where they have learnt that Will Stutely is to hang.

Will Stutely is marched out of the castle, surrounded by guards. He begs the Sheriff to be allowed an honourable death with a sword in his hand as his 'noble master'

– Robin – 'nere a man that yet was hang'd on the tree'. But the Sheriff is adamant that he is going to be hanged. Will even offers to fight empty-handed, but the Sheriff swears that he is going to hang, along with his master. Will curses him, saying that if ever the Sheriff meets his master, he will be made to pay for what he has done.

As Will is led to the gallows, Little John leaps from the bushes, cuts the rope around Will's hands and takes a sword from one of the Sheriff's men. Back to back, they fight off the Sheriff's men until Robin and his archers turn up. As the arrows fly, the Sheriff flees, followed by his men. Then Stutely rejoins the Merry Men in the safety of the forest.

Arthur á Bland

Although there were said to be between twenty and seven score (140) Merry Men, few others are named. Arthur á Bland turns up in *Robin Hood and the Tanner*, which appeared on the Stationers' Registry on 17 April 1657 but seems to be considerably older. In some versions of the ballad, Arthur á Bland is Little John's cousin and a tanner by trade. One summer morning, he goes out into the greenwood to hunt deer, when he espies Robin Hood.

Robin asks him what business he has in the forest and accuses him of being a thief who has come to steal the King's deer. In a curious reversal of the normal situation, Robin claims to be the keeper of the parish. 'The King hath a-put me in trust,' he says, and tells the tanner to get on his way. But the tanner refuses to go and defends himself with a staff. The fight continues for more than two hours. Unable to beat the tanner, Robin sounds his bugle horn and Little John comes running.

'What is the matter?' asks Little John, observing that Robin is not doing so well.

'Here's a tanner so good,' says Robin, 'I warrant he's tanned my hide.'

'If he is such a good tanner,' says Little John, 'we should have another bout, and I warrant he'll tan my hide too.'

Robin tells Little John there is no need for that, particularly as he is 'of thine blood'. Little John throws away his staff and embraces Arthur. Then the three of them hold hands and dance around an oak tree. They vow to live as one.

David of Doncaster

David of Doncaster appears in *Robin Hood and the Golden Arrow*. He warns Robin against going to the Sheriff of Nottingham's archery contest, fearing it may be a trap.

'Thou smells of a coward,' says Robin. 'Thy words does not please me.'

And he resolves to go anyway.

Robin and his Merry Men then abandon their Lincoln green and dress in white, blue, yellow, brown. Robin himself is in red. The prize is to be an arrow with a gold head and a shaft made of silver. Robin wins, but this is not good enough. He wants the Sheriff to know that he has taken the arrow. Little John suggests that Robin write a letter. Then he would deliver it by attaching it to an arrow and firing it into town.

10

MAID MARIAN AND FRIAR TUCK

Maid Marian

Although Little John, Will Scarlet and Much the miller's son appear in the early ballads of Robin Hood, he has no female companion. He is devoted, instead, to the Virgin Mary. The first mention of Maid Marian comes in Alexander Barclay's series of poems known as *The Ship of Follies* written around 1508. It says:

> Yet would I gladly hear some merry fytte
> Of Maid Marian, or else of Robin Hood.

This is taken to mean that Maid Marian comes from a different tradition than Robin Hood and plays no part in the original legend. Indeed, around 1283 the French poet

Adam de la Halle wrote '*Le Jeu de Robin et Marion*' (The Play of Robin and Marion), a dramatization of a medieval French pastoral poem. However, the Robin here is not our Robin Hood. He is not an outlaw and not an archer. He is simply the peasant lover of the shepherdess Marion. The story seems to have been a traditional French folktale and appeared again in '*Mirour de l'homme*' (Mirror of Mankind) by John Gower, an English poet writing in French, in 1380. In it, Robin and Marion participate in rustic festivals and condemn the revels of the monks.

By 1392, the *Jeu* was being performed in Angers in France around Whitsun or Pentecost. In the May games around that time there was a figure called 'Murrian'. But this appears to have been the 'Moorish one' who appeared with a blackened face. However, in the records kept in Kingston from 1509 a costume was provided for a Marian. At first, she appears to be Friar Tuck's girlfriend rather than Robin's. And as the paramour of a wayward friar it is fairly clear that she was not a maid. Later, though, Robin and Marian take over the games as king and queen of the May.

By the Munday plays, Robin's lover is Matilda Fitzwater, but she also appears as Marian and she disappears into the forest to escape the predations of the lecherous King John. Fulk FitzWarin's Matilda suffered in the same way. Matilda was also the name of the wife of Robert Hood of Wakefield, one of the candidates to be the real Robin Hood. Matilda Fitzwater's surname is sometimes rendered as Fitzwalter and her father as Robert Fitzwalter, who rebelled against King John and was one of the barons charged with enforcing the Magna Carta. He was exiled and outlawed. The tale of King John's attempted seduction of his eldest daughter Maud, or Matilda, became a popular subject for romance.

Munday says that Matilda is 'chaste', so she is a maid in the sense of being a virgin. The name Marian means literally 'of Mary', reflecting Robin's earlier devotion to the Virgin Mary.

There are passing references to Marian in the ballads *Robin Hood and Queen Katherine*, written around 1630 or before, and *Robin Hood's Golden Prize*, written around 1650. But she only takes a starring role in *Robin Hood and Maid Marian*, thought to have been written after the Restoration of Charles II in 1660. By this time she has become 'a bonny fine maid of noble degree'. She is said to be more beautiful than 'Queen Hellen' (presumably Helen of Troy, the most beautiful woman in ancient Greece), Rosamond, the mistress of Henry II, and Jane Shore, the mistress of Edward IV.

By then Robin is 'the earl of Huntington, nobly born'. When he takes to the forest, she disguises herself as a page and – armed with bow, sword and buckler – goes into the greenwood after him. They meet but do not recognize each other and begin to fight.

In a sword fight that lasts for over an hour, Robin's face is blooded. Marian is also wounded. Robin calls a halt and, as usual, invites his foe to join his Merry Men. She immediately recognizes his voice and they kiss and embrace. The ballad ends there. They do not marry and live happily ever after. In fact, Robin marries someone else according to *Robin Hood's Birth, Breeding, Valour, and Marriage*, written around 1681–4. Robin, from Locksly in Nottinghamshire, outshoots Adam Bell, Clim of the Clugh and William a Clowsdeslé. His uncle is Gamwell, of Great Gamwell Hall. In the forest, Robin meets

Clorinda, queen of the shepherds, who is already kitted out in a green velvet gown with boots that reach up to her knee. 'Her gait was graceful, her body was straight.' Her hair and eyebrows are black. Her skin is 'smooth as glass', and her face 'spoke wisdom and modesty too'.

She is carrying a bow and arrows. When Robin asks where she is going, she says 'to kill a fat buck'. Robin asks her to accompany him into a nearby bower where she can sit down and rest. But as they near the bower they see two hundred bucks. She picks out the fattest and shoots it. Robin is impressed by a woman who can kill her own venison and asks her to feast with him. She asks Robin his name, then, after a few words of conversation, he asks her to be his bride. She blushes at the notion, then, after a short pause, agrees. The following day they marry at Titbury, before retiring to bed. But this is the last we hear of Clorinda.

There is a local tradition that Robin and Marian married in St Mary's church in Edwinstowe, which is in Sherwood. It is entirely possible that the church was built around 1175. There was an earlier church on the site that dates from 633. The priest there might even have been one of the Merry Men. In 1334, the vicar of Edwinstow, John de Roystan, was convicted of 'venison trespass' – killing the King's deer. However, the marriage of Robin and Marian does not appear in the literature and the idea of a chaste affair between the couple persists.

Nevertheless we do know that the Robert Hood of Wakefield, who Joseph Hunter put forward as a candidate for the real Robin, was married and his wife's name was Matilda. Hunter also made a connection between Matilda and the Prioress of Kirkees who, with her lover Sir Roger of Doncaster, was supposed to have killed Robin.

Although it has always been assumed that the Prioress was Robin's cousin, the *Gest of Robyn Hode* only says that she 'was of his kin'.

According to the *Gest*, Robin remained in the King's service only for fifteen months before growing homesick and returning to Sherwood, where he lived for another 22 years before his death. If he entered Edward III's service in November 1323, following the King's visit to Nottingham, he would have left in early 1325. That means that he would have died in 1347. Hunter sought to establish that the Prioress at the time was Elizabeth de Staynton. She was certainly Prioress at one time as her grave was discovered 18 yards from the east end of the priory church in 1706, and an illustration of the grave slab appeared in the 1785 revised edition of William Camden's *Britannia*. However, the slab was undated and it had previously been thought that she had been Prioress in the thirteenth century.

Hunter claimed to have found documentation showing that Elizabeth's guardian William de Notton sought to have her removed from the convent, but her mother objected and money was paid from her father's estate to cover her upkeep. This carried on for the first 20 years of Edward III's 50-year reign, so from 1327 to 1347. In one of the later ballads, *Robin Hood's Garland*, the Prioress was said to have committed suicide after betraying Robin. It was later discovered that Margaret de Savile was Prioress in 1348, though she was only officially appointed to the post by the Archbishop of York in 1350, which means that she must have been only acting Prioress in 1348, stepping into the breach, perhaps, following the unexpected death or dismissal of the previous incumbent. According to the Wakefield Manor Rolls, Alice de Scriven was Prioress until 1331. Elizabeth was already a nun in the convent at that time and, if Hunter is right, she seems to have taken over as Prioress from 1331 to 1347.

John Walker, the author of the 1973 book *The True History of Robin Hood*, said he found a document in Woolly Hall, near Wakefield, which said: 'On John de Staynton's death his widow Joan married Hugh de Toothill, of Toothill, near Rasterick.' This confirms Hunter's tale that Elizabeth's mother had married again. Two of her four daughters had married her new husband's son, while the other two, one of whom was Elizabeth, were sent to the priory at Kirklees.

Hugh de Toothill had a daughter named Matilda who appears on the Wakefield Manor Rolls in 1314, when she was fined for taking firewood without permission from the estate. The only other Matilda that appears on the Wakefield Manor Roll at the time is Robert Hood's wife Matilda. On Toothill's marriage to Joan Staynton, Matilda Hood would have become Elizabeth Staynton's stepsister, so Robert and Elizabeth would have become kin. She was his sister-in-law.

Friar Tuck

Friar Tuck made his first appearance in the May games in association with May Marian, or the Lady of May, who was a far less chaste figure than the virginal Maid Marian. He appears in *Robin Hood and the Golden Prize* alongside Marian. In that ballad, Robin too disguises himself as a friar. Friar Tuck also shows up in *Robin Hood and Queen Katherine*.

The first Queen Catherine in England was the wife of Henry V (1413–22), but they were together in England for less than six months. Only a brief period was spent in

London – the ballad maintains that they attended an archery contest on Finsbury Field. Consequently, it is thought that the Queen Katherine of the ballad was one of the three wives of Henry VIII (1491–1547) named Catherine. However, after Henry's divorce from his first wife Catherine of Aragon in 1533 and the Dissolution of the Monasteries between 1536 and 1540, jolly Friars were no longer popular figures – though they may have been outlaws. On the other hand, Friar Tuck could not have been one of Robin Hood's Merry Men if Robin was around in the reign of Richard I as friars did not reach England until 1224.

Friars were men of certain religious orders, particularly the mendicants: Augustinians, Carmelites, Dominicans and Franciscans. They spent their time wandering the country spreading the Christian word. According to Chaucer and Langland, they were famously corrupt. However, they were close to the common people, not like the monks who lived behind closed doors or abbots and bishops who mixed with the aristocracy. So it would be no surprise to find a friar among an outlaw band, particularly one dedicated to stealing from the upper echelons of the Church.

The name Friar Tuck made an early appearance in the history of criminality. In 1417, two royal writs mention a man named Friar Tuck. He had gathered around him a gang of outlaws who had committed a series of robberies and murders across Sussex and Surrey. They had entered the chases and warrens of the two counties to hunt without a licence, threatened the foresters and warreners, and burnt their lodges. The writs commissioned men to catch Friar Tuck and his men. They had little luck as Tuck and his band were still at large twelve years later, according to a letter of 1429. However, Friar Tuck was identified as Robert Stafford, the chaplain of Lindfield, Sussex. His alias was still a bit of a puzzle to royal officials though. It seems they had never heard it before. One of the writs said that the outlaw had 'assumed the name of Frere Tuk newly so called in common parlance'. The other said he had taken 'the unusual name, in common parlance, of Frere Tuk'. Interestingly, Lindfield is just five miles from Fletching where the surname Robynhod was first recorded in 1296.

Friar Tuck appears in a fragment of the play about the outlaw, sometimes called *Robin Hood and the Knight* or *Robin Hood and the Sheriff*, though the main outline of the story comes from the ballad *Robin Hood and Guy of Gisborne*. It is thought to have been written around 1475. In it 'ffrere Tuke' is one of Robin's band who take on the Sheriff's men when Robin is in jail. The outlaws are captured and Robin is brought out to be hanged, but Robin and the outlaws escape, perhaps with the help of Friar Tuck.

An earlier version of this story appears as a May game play, printed in 1560 alongside another play adapting an older ballad *Robin Hood and the Potter*. At the end of that play, Robin offers Friar Tuck a woman as incentive to join the band – May game versions of the story were inevitably bawdier. Although unnamed, many scholars have assumed that the woman was meant to be Marian. She was sometimes pictured as the friar's dancing partner, elsewhere he was her confessor.

The sixteenth-century morality play *Magnificence* written by John Skelton (1460–1529) talks of a man being made like 'Friar Tuck, To preach out of a pillory hole, Without an anthem or a stole'. The 1537 play *Thersites* mentions 'as tall a man as Friar Tuck' in the context of a fight. In the *Two Gentlemen of Verona*, written in the early 1590s, Shakespeare makes an illusion to 'the bare scalp of Robin Hood's far friar'. And he is mentioned in Anthony Munday's play *The Downfall of Robert Earl of Huntington* in 1598.

The story of Robin Hood's first encounter with Friar Tuck seems to relate back to the ballad *Robin Hood and the Curtal Friar* – the oldest surviving copies of this have been dated to the seventeenth century though there are reasons to believe that the ballad dates from the fifteenth century. In it, the friar is not named. However, there is good reason to believe that this is Friar Tuck.

Curtal is an old form of the word 'curtailed' and a curtal friar is one who wears a short habit. The Franciscans particularly were known for their short habits, worn on the instructions of St Francis himself. They were 'curtalled', or curtailed, by a cord around the waist. Other mendicant orders followed suit. But the word curtal has other meanings. It was used as a term of opprobrium for someone who is short or dumpy, as Friar Tuck is often portrayed. A rogue who wears a short cloak was also referred to as a curtal, as was a criminal who had had their ears docked in the pillory, a common punishment for theft or sedition. A curtal was also another name for a drab – a dirty or untidy woman, a slut or even a prostitute.

In the ballad the protagonist is also referred to as a 'cutted friar', meaning that his habit has been cut short or trimmed. There is the same implication in the name 'tuck', in the sense of a pleat in a garment used to shorten it. Franciscans wore their habits tucked or pleated by the cord around their waists. So it is reasonable to assume that the curtal friar and Friar Tuck are one and the same. The word 'tuck' meaning food is of a much later origin.

Although Robin Hood is plainly a hero in medieval England, in the ballads he is often bested by Little John, the Potter, the Monk or whoever else he comes up against. This time he is confronted by a wily man of the cloth.

Two versions of *Robin Hood and the Curtal Friar* exist. One begins with the usual celebration of the month of May. Then half a page is missing. Robin says that he will neither eat nor drink until he has seen the 'cutted friar'. He heads for Fountain Abbey, a Cistercian monastery near Ripon, north Yorkshire, though it is referred to in the text as a nunnery. Near the abbey, he hides his men in a brake of fern, telling them to come and find him if they hear him blow on his horn.

Along the way, he meets a friar armed with a sword and buckler. Robin asks the friar to carry him over 'this wild water'. The friar carries Robin on his back, but when they get to the other side, he draws his sword and demands that the outlaw carry him back. When they reach the bank, the now sodden Robin asks the friar to carry him across the water once more. Then more of the manuscript is missing. When it resumes, Robin's men have turned up.

The friar says that, as he allowed Robin to blow on his horn, he must be allowed to whistle. Robin says he sees no harm in this, but when the friar whistles 'halfe a hundred good bandoggs' turn up – these are dogs so savage that they are usually kept chained. The friar then says: 'Every dogg to a man . . . And I my selfe to Robin Hood.'

Robin replies: 'Every God's forbott [God forfend] . . . That ever soe shold bee, I had rather be matched with three of the tikes [dogs], Ere I wold be matched on thee.'

That the friar depends on dogs might indicate in the medieval mind that he was a Dominican – or *Dominicanes* in Latin. With a play on the words, *Domini canes* would mean the hounds of God.

Robin then offers his friendship if the friar will call off his dogs. The friar whistles again and the dogs lay down. He asks what Robin wants, and Robin invites him to go to the merry greenwood.

The other version, dating from 1660, is called *The famous Battel between Robin Hood and the Curtall Friar; To a new Northern Tune*. It begins in the summer time, when the leaves are green and the flowers are in bloom. The Merry Men are practising their archery – Will Scadlock, Midge and Little John all kill deer at a range of 500 feet. Robin is impressed and says he would ride a hundred miles to find anyone that could match them. Will laughs and says that there is a curtal friar that lives in Fountains Abbey that could be at all of them. Robin swears a solemn oath that he will not eat or drink until he has seen the friar.

Robin then heads off to Fountain Dale. There is a Fountain Dale near Mansfield in Nottinghamshire though, apparently, it was not named until after the ballad appeared. On the way, he meets a curtal friar walking by the riverside. He is heavily armed with a helmet, as well as a broadsword and buckler. Again Robin asks the friar to carry him over the water and the friar takes him on his back. Then the friar gets Robin to carry him back. Robin insists that the friar carry him across once more, but in the middle to the stream the friar throws him in.

Both swim to shore. Robin takes his bow and fires an arrow at the friar, which the friar fends off with his buckler. Robin fires off all his arrows to no avail, then a sword fight begins. They fight from ten in the morning until four in the afternoon. By this time, Robin is on his knees and he begs the friar for a favour – he wants to be allowed to blow three blasts on his horn. When he does so, fifty yeomen appear.

The friar then asks for a favour for himself. He wants to whistle three times. When he does, fifty dogs turn up. 'Here's for every man a dog, And I my self for thee,' says the friar.

Two dogs attack Robin – one from in front; one behind – and tear off his mantle of Lincoln green. The Merry Men fire on the dogs, but they are so well trained that they can catch arrows in their mouths.

Little John then stepped in and asked the friar to call off the dogs – otherwise, he said, he would kill both the dogs and the friar. He made his point by drawing his bow and killing ten of the friar's dogs. The friar then asks Little John to stop while he discusses the matter with his master – Robin.

Robin asks the friar to give up Fountain Dale and go to Nottingham with him because he is a good fighting man. In seven years, 'neither knight, lord, nor earl' has made him yield before. So here Friar Tuck is depicted as a great swordsman. Elsewhere he is an archer. It is only later on that he becomes a jovial, glutton with a great love of ale, who is employed in the stories as comic relief.

11

THE SHERIFF OF NOTTINGHAM AND SIR GUY OF GISBORNE

The Sheriff of Nottingham

The Sheriff of Nottingham is the principal villain in the tale of Robin Hood. When Robin goes to pray to the Virgin Mary at the church of St Mary's in Nottingham in *Robin Hood and the Monk*, the Sheriff spots him as the 'kynggis felon' and has him arrested. He also appears as the antagonist in *A Gest of Robyn Hode* and in the earliest surviving play *Robyn Hod and the Shryff of Notyngham*, thought to have derived from the earlier ballad *Robin Hood and Guy of Gisborne*. And he appears in *Robin and the Potter*.

The Sheriff of Nottingham is not named in any of the texts and there are a number of competing theories about who he could be. One of them is that he is William de Wendenal who was High Sheriff of Nottinghamshire and Derbyshire from 1191 to 1194, the period when Richard I was away in the Holy Land. He was thought to have been of Norman descent, whose family came over to England with William the Conqueror in 1066. He was plainly trusted by Richard. But when Richard returned in March 1194, William de Ferrers, the fourth earl of Derby, took over his position and de Wendenal disappears from the record. However, in the *Gest*, Robin kills the sheriff before the King returns to Nottingham.

In medieval England, the sheriff was the king's representative in a county. The civil law was in the hands of the barons, but they usually left its enforcement to the knights who occupied the various manors on their estates. The barons only intervened when a punishment of execution or permanent disablement was imposed as it would deprive them of a worker or a soldier in time of war when troops had to be raised. The knights usually left the villagers to their own devices as long as dues were paid and basic order was maintained. Beyond that, local disputes were left to the Church to resolve.

In the towns and cities, the guilds policed the local trading laws, bringing complaints before the weekly meeting of the council who levied fines. Criminal matters were brought before the assizes, a special monthly meetings of the council. As there were no full-time police or law-enforcement officers, the council deputized a local watch to arrest anyone they wished to question or to prosecute. Minor crimes were punished by the stocks or pillory. Convicted criminals were put on display in the town square, perhaps with a stolen object tied around their neck. Passersby would pelt them with rotten fruit or vegetables – or sometimes solid objects, though rocks and stones were forbidden. For more serious crimes, criminals would go to the whipping post or the gallows. There were jails, but these were not usually for long-term punishment. They were lockups where prisoners were beaten, starved or tortured until the authorities decided what to do with them. Normally, for a comparatively minor crime, an offender would be mutilated or branded and sent on their way.

Thing did improve slightly when prison building was started following the Assize of Clarendon in 1166. They were privately run and inmates had to pay for their upkeep. Gaolers were particularly harsh on those who did not pay up. In 1290, the gaoler at Newgate bound a prisoner so tightly with irons that his neck and spine were broken and at Sarum gaol in 1384 the gaoler kept a prisoner in the stocks so long one winter that his feet rotted away.

There was no standing army, though barons were supposed to supply troops for the king's use. All adult males were supposed to practise archery on a Sunday afternoon. Those who did not turn up were fined. A sheriff would be supplied with a contingent of troops. His job was to collect taxes from the county he administered, supply the king's messengers with an armed escort and put down any local unrest, and he would be housed in one of the many castles the Normans built.

Although the sheriff was the representative of the authority of the Crown in a county, the barons took little notice. However, to ordinary people, his power was absolute. But his writ could only run so far. Outside the villages and towns there was little protection for people or property. Generally travellers were wealthy people who could afford to pay for an escort. There was little point in poor people travelling from place to place hoping to better themselves. Outsiders were viewed with suspicion.

Those who broke the law and failed to answer the charges laid against them were declared outlaw – that is, outside the protection of the law. Their property was impounded. In the fourteenth century, little of England had been cleared for crops and much of the country was still heavily forested. So outlaws simply took to the woods. Few attempts were made to track them down. It was an impossible task. A few men with bows and arrows concealed in the trees could pick off armoured troops. After civil wars or rebellions, the danger would increase as trained men from the losing side would hide out in the forests. Once outlawed, their own means of survival was theft. Despite having the odds stacked against him, it was the sheriff's duty to round up these renegades.

With Richard I out of the country, the sheriff's job would have been a particularly unpopular one. Richard's brother John stirred up discontent with his efforts to usurp the throne. Then, when Richard was held hostage by Duke Leopold V of Austria and the Holy Roman Emperor Henry VI from 1192 to 1194, the Queen Mother, Eleanor of Aquitaine, had to raise a ransom of 150,000 marks, a considerable burden for the taxpayers of England. Sheriffs were often corrupt on their own account. In the fourteenth century, Sir Richard Ingram, then Sheriff of Nottingham and Derbyshire, was in league with the notorious Coterel gang. John de Oxenford, Sheriff from 1334 to 1338, was charged with extortion.

William de Ferrers who took over from William de Wendenal in 1194, supported Richard against his brother John, besieging Nottingham Castle which was being held by John's supporters in March 1194. However, when John became king in 1199, de Ferrers became a great favourite.

Another candidate for Robin Hood's Sheriff of Nottingham was Roger de Lacy. In 1191, he had been entrusted with Tickhill and Nottingham castles and hanged two knights who conspired to surrender them. During John's reign, his landholding increased considerably.

William Brewer became Sheriff of Nottingham and Derbyshire in 1196. He had been one of the justiciars appointed to run the country when Richard I was away at the crusade. Under John he became one of the most powerful men in the country. He sat in the Exchequer into the reign of Henry III. As well as being Sheriff of Nottingham and Derbyshire, he became Sheriff of Berkshire, Cornwall, Devon, Dorset, Hampshire, Oxfordshire, Somerset, Sussex and Wiltshire. There are indications that he was corrupt. He was often very unpopular with the people in the counties he administered. The men of Somerset, Dorset and Cornwall paid the King money to have him removed. During his lifetime he amassed large estates and had over sixty knights under his command. He also founded three monasteries.

Other authorities have suggested that the Sheriff of Nottingham concerned was Philip Mark, who was Sheriff of Nottinghamshire and Derbyshire from 1221 to 1226 or Brian de Lisle, who was chief forester of Nottinghamshire and Derbyshire from 1209 to 1217, chief justice of the forest from 1221 to 1224 and Sheriff of Yorkshire from 1233 to 1234.

Then there is Eustace of Lowdham, who was Sheriff of Yorkshire form 29 April 1225 to 26 May 1226, then deputy Sheriff until Michaelmas that year. He was also forest justice north of the Trent in 1226 and Sheriff of

Nottinghamshire from 1232 to 1233. As deputy Sheriff of Yorkshire, he had to collect the penalties imposed by Robert de Lexinton, who had outlawed Robert Hod in the York assizes in 1225. Eustace would have had to account for the 32 shillings and 6 pence raised by the sale of Hod's chattels at the Michaelmas Exchequer of 1226. He is the only Sheriff of Nottingham who had any known connection to an outlaw that could have been Robin Hood.

However, if the *Gest* is correct and Edward was on the throne at the time, the Sheriff of Nottingham in question would be the one in office on 9 November 1323, when the King paid a visit. Sir Henry de Faucumberg was Sheriff of Nottinghamshire at that time. It was his second term of office. He had been Sheriff from November 1318 to November 1319, then again between June 1323 and March 1325. What's more, he was not just Sheriff of Nottinghamshire and Derbyshire, but Sheriff of Yorkshire as well – between April 1325 and September 1327, and again from 1328 to 1330.

Again, if Robin was pardoned and joined the King's service in November 1323, then left fifteen months later as in the *Gest*, he would have returned to Barnsdale early in 1325. This is exactly the time Faucumberg is transferred from Nottinghamshire to Yorkshire. Perhaps the King feared that Robin would renew his criminal – if not treasonous – activities and wanted a reliable man on the spot in case there was trouble. In March 1326, Faucumberg was instructed to hunt down a gang lead by Eustace de Folville, who might well have had some connection to Robin.

Faucumberg himself was a Yorkshireman. He was the second son of William de Faucumberg of Catfoss in the East Riding of Yorkshire. His elder brother John should have inherited, but when William died in January 1295, Henry took over. According to the Manor Rolls of Wakefield, he acquired a large estate in Holderness. But things did not seem to go right for him. On 12 March 1313, the Manor Rolls record that he stole wood from the barn of the Earl of Warenne. He was fined for a similar offence on 4 October 1314. On 27 March 1315, he was held in contempt of court for refusing to take the oath. He was up for theft again on 18 October 1315. Then things must have turned around for him. Three years later he was Sheriff of Nottingham.

During the dip in his fortunes, Faucumberg was in Wakefield along with the Robert Hood and his wife Matilda who appear in the court rolls in 1316 and 1317. Faucumberg was also one of those who put down the Lancastrian revolt at Boroughbridge in 1322, linking back to Hunter's theory that Robin and his men had been outlawed because they were Contrariants – followers of Thomas, earl of Lancaster in his rebellion against Edward II. He was also put in charge of seizing the Contrariants' land, some of which he kept for himself.

Sir Henry de Faucumberg makes an excellent candidate for Robin Hood's arch adversary. He was Sheriff of Nottinghamshire when the King visited in November 1323 and was Sheriff of Yorkshire when Robin Hood was thought to have returned to Barnsdale in 1325. Seizing the Contrariants' lands would have made him extremely unpopular and he would have been an easy target for ballad writers. He also had an older brother named John who was dispossessed. According to the *Gest*, Little John came from Holderness, where Henry de Faucumberg had an estate. No further record has been found of his elder brother John.

Guy of Gisborne

Robin Hood and Guy of Gisborne introduces a second villain, after the Sheriff of Nottingham. The ballad exists in a single seventeenth-century copy, but is thought to be much older, possibly dating from 1475. It begins, like *Robin Hood and the Monk*, with a few lines praising the greenwood. Then Robin relates a dream he has had where he was beaten and tied up by two yeomen who took his bow. Robin and Little John then set out to find the yeoman and exact revenge. They come across a stranger leaning against a tree. He is dressed in horse-hide and is armed with a sword and a dagger.

Little John volunteers to challenge the stranger. Robin high-handedly refuses his offer and Little John returns to Barnsdale. There he finds that two of the outlaws have been slain and Will Scarlet is on the run from the Sheriff. Little John takes a potshot at one of the Sheriff's men, but his bow breaks. The Sheriff's men then seize Little John and tie him to a tree to await execution.

Meanwhile, Robin has approached the stranger who is now identified as Sir Guy of Gisborne. They exchange greetings. Sir Guy says he is lost and Robin offers to be his guide. Guy then reveals that he is seeking an outlaw – 'men call him Robin Hood'. Before they part, Robin and Guy hold an archery competition, which Robin wins. Guy then wants to know more about his opponent and asks him his name.

'My name is Robin Hood of Barnsdale,' says Robin. 'A fellow thou hast long sought.'

They draw their swords and set to. The fight goes on for two hours until Robin stumbles and is wounded. He calls on Our Lady for help. Invigorated, he leaps to his feet and slays Gisborne. Then we see a vicious side to

Robin that we have not seen before. He takes Guy's head by the hair and sticks it on the end of his bow. Then he takes a knife and mutilates his face so that 'no one of a woman born' could recognize him.

Robin then dons Guy's horse-hide suit and heads back to Barnsdale. On the ways, he blows Guy's horn, announcing to the Sheriff that he has slain Robin Hood. The Sheriff asks him to name his reward, but Robin, disguised as Gisborne, refuses gold, saying that, as he had slain the master, now he will slay the knave – Little John:

> This is all the reward I aske,
> Nor no other will I have.

The Sheriff thinks that he is mad, but grants his request. At the same time, Little John recognizes Robin's voice and knows he is about to be saved.

Robin asks the Sheriff's men to stand back so that he can hear Little John's Confession. He then cuts Little John loose and gives him Gisborne's bow. The Sheriff, seeing Little John aiming at him, takes flight, followed by his men. But the Sheriff cannot run away fast enough and Little John's broad arrow 'did cleave his heart in twain'.

Robin Hood and Guy of Gisborne shows a darker side to Robin. Life was cheap in the twelfth century and an outlaw would have to be prepared to kill or be killed. Certainly he could not expect any mercy if he were caught – especially not from the Sheriff of Nottinghan or Guy of Gisborne. Men who took to the forest with other outcasts would become quickly inured to the sight of bloodshed and slaughter. Robin is equally savage in the later ballad *Robin Hood's Progress to Nottingham*, also published under the name *Robin and the Forresters*. In it, Robin is challenged to an archery contest by fifteen foresters. He wins it by killing a deer at a distance of 100 rods (550 yards or 503 metres) and breaking two or three ribs. When they refuse to pay up, Robin kills fourteen of them with his bow and arrow. The fifteenth, the man who began the quarrel, tries to run away. Robin trains his bow and arrow on him and forces him to return.

'You said I was no archer,' says Robin. 'But say so now again.'

Then he fires the arrow that 'split his head in twain'.

The people of Nottingham try to arrest Robin for killing the foresters, many of whom they knew. But Robin fights them off – 'some lost legs, and some lost arms, and some did lose their blood'. Then Robin takes up his 'noble bow' and returns to the greenwood, while the foresters' bodies are carried into Nottingham for burial in the churchyard.

In *Robin Hood and Guy of Gisborne*, both Robin and Guy are introduced as yeomen. But in later versions of the tale, Gisborne becomes Sir Guy. Disinherited knights hired themselves out as mercenaries during time of war during the Middle Ages. In peacetime, they became bounty hunters like Guy, who expects to get 'forty pounds in golde' for tracking down Robin.

Guy of Gisborne's name is also spelt Gisbourne, Gisburne, Gysborne or Gisborn. He is thought to be from Gisburn in Lancashire, which is just beyond Skipton on the edge of the Yorkshire Dales, but there is no surviving record of a Sir Guy living there.

Other villains

There are other villains in the tale of Robin Hood. One of them is Sir Roger of Doncaster, the Prioress's lover in the

Gest, who is clearly also the 'Red Roger' responsible for Robin's demise in *The Death of Robin Hood*. The Wakefield Manor Rolls list a Roger de Doncaster as the chief steward to the earl of Warenne, the owner of Wakefield Manor before the earl of Lancaster took over the estate. And a court held in Wakefield on 22 January 1327 ordered that eight acres of land at Crigglestone be given to Roger, son of William of Doncaster. This makes him a contemporary of Robert Hood in Wakefield. His name also appeared as a witness to the deeds of the manor of Hornington, eight miles south-west of York. It describes Roger of Doncaster as a chaplain.

If the Prioress of Kirklees had a lover, he would have to have been someone who could enter and leave a convent without suspicion – a clergyman perhaps. There is even evidence that there was something amiss at Kirklees priory. The Archbishop of York's Register for 10 October 1315 mentions that the archbishop had heard 'scandalous reports' about the nuns at Kirklees.

Roger of Doncaster was no angel either. In 1306, he was sent by the Archbishop of York to be priest at the church in Ruddington near Nottingham. According to the records, he was still the parish priest there in 1328. However, in 1333, he was imprisoned for a time for trespassing in Sherwood Forest. What's more, Roger the chaplain also seems to have been a knight – and a knight with a chequered sexual history. In June 1309, a 'Sir Roger de Doncastria' was charged with adultery with Agnes, the wife of Philip de Pavely.

Everything here seems to fit. This Roger of Doncaster is a knight who, as a clergyman, would have access to the convent at Kirklees. He has connections with Wakefield, Nottingham and Sherwood. He was not a man who obeyed his vows of chastity and seems to have been the type who was up for sexual adventure – with a nun, perhaps.

However, if he had been old enough to be a parish priest in 1306, he must have been at least 60 in 1347. Robin himself would have been getting on a bit by then, so the final swordfight that led to both their deaths would hardly have been the athletic, all-action affair portrayed in the movies.

12

KING RICHARD AND KING JOHN

The other enduring villain of the modern tale of Robin Hood is King John, or rather Prince John, count of Mortain, who tried to usurp the throne while his elder brother King Richard was out of the country from 1191 to 1194 and finally succeeded him in 1199. However, it was only the Scottish historian John Major, writing in 1521, that placed Robin Hood in that time frame. The *Gest* says that Robin was active in the reign of King Edward. It is Andrew Munday's *The Downfall of Robert, Earle of Huntington* that puts Robin in the reign of King John. It seems that, in searching for a villain, Munday borrowed heavily from the anonymous play *The Troublesome Reign of King John*.

King John had also been portrayed as a villain in the *Fouke le Fitz Waryn* and the tale of Eustace the Monk. There have been worse kings, but John has to stand comparison with his supposedly virtuous brother and great British hero, the crusader Richard the Lion-Heart. But, then, they came from a troubled family.

Early life

Their father was Henry II who spent just 14 years of his 34-year reign in England. During that time he obtained the homage of the Scottish kings and took back Northumberland from them. Pope Adrian IV (1154–9), the only English pope, gave Henry the right to rule Ireland, while the marriages of his three daughters gave him influence in Germany, Sicily and Castile. However, he was also responsible for the murder of Thomas Becket, known to history as Thomas à Becket, Archbishop of Canterbury, in 1170, in a tussle over the division of power between church and state.

In 1152, Henry had married Eleanor of Aquitance, the estranged wife of Louis VII of France (1137–80). Along with three daughters, she gave him four sons – Henry, Geoffrey, Richard and John. The boys fell out due to Henry II's habit of ostensibly dividing his possessions among his sons, while reserving real power for himself. He even had his eldest son Henry crowned co-regent. Although he was known as Henry the Young King, he exercised no real power, but, by having him betrothed to Louis VII's daughter Margaret when he was only three, Henry II used him to breach the rift with Louis. The dowry would be the town of Vexin that lay on the border between English-held Normandy and France. With a special dispensation from the pope, they were married two years later. And in 1172, Margaret was crowned queen of England.

Henry fell out with his father when the King tried to find territories for his fourth son John – nicknamed *Sans Terre* or Lackland – at the expense of his brother Geoffrey. Richard supported his two older brothers, as did Eleanor. The rebellion was supported by numerous barons, and the kings of Scotland and France. Henry II defeated them one by one over the next year. He imprisoned Eleanor and persuaded the papal legate to annul their marriage. Henry II had had illegitimate children during his marriage, but he now publicly acknowledged his new mistress, the 'Fair Rosamund' – Rosamund Clifford. The chronicler Gerald of Wales records that Henry 'having long been a secret adulterer, now openly flaunted his mistress, not that rose of the world [*rosa-mundi*] of false and frivolous renown, but that rose of unchastity [*rosa-immundi*]'.

Henry II was reconciled with his sons, but Eleanor remained in custody until he died. There were further fallings-out though. When the King gave Aquitaine to his son Henry, Richard, who had inherited the duchy from his mother at the age of 11, rebelled. Henry died in 1183 and Aquitaine was passed to John, spreading further discord among the brothers. Geoffrey allied with Philip II Augustus of France (1179–1223), who had succeeded his father Louis. However, after boasting that he and the French king were going to devastate Normandy, Geoffrey died in a accident at a tournament in Paris in 1186. Richard replaced him as Philip's ally and, it is thought, his homosexual lover. They defeated Henry II, who died near Tours on 6 July 1189 after hearing that John had also joined his enemies. Richard, who had harried his dying father until he named him heir, succeeded him as duke of Normandy. Two months later, he was crowned King of England. One of his first acts was to release his mother.

King Richard

Although Richard I (1189–99) is one of England's most famous kings, he had little English blood in him, did not speak the language and spent less than six months of his ten-year reign in the country. He regarded the country as little more than a source of revenue for his crusade.

'I would have sold London itself if I could have found a rich enough buyer,' he said. Many towns benefited from the royal charters he gave them in return for their financial assistance.

Henry II had promised to undertake a crusade as expiation for the murder of Thomas Becket. This was not an altogether disinterested pledge and the Angevins had acquired title to the crusader kingdom of Jerusalem by marriage. Unable to acquit his pledge, Henry had bequeathed it to Richard, whose prowess on the battle-field had already earned him the sobriquet *Coeur de Lion* – 'Lion-Heart' or 'Lion-Hearted'. He had gained this reputation because of the ruthlessness with which he put down revolts in his French possessions. In 1179 he had taken what was thought to be the impregnable castle of Taillebourg in Saintonge.

When Richard took the throne, preparations were being made for the Third Crusade after Saladin had captured Jerusalem in 1187. He was determined to join, but first he secured Normandy and Anjou. Open war against France was averted when Philip also decided to join the Crusade. As soon as Richard had raised an army, he headed for the Holy Land, leaving England in the hands of his mother, the newly freed Eleanor of Aquitaine, who held it against the intrigues of his brother John.

Richard was no soft touch. On his way to the Third Crusade, he made a law against thieving sailors. It said: 'Whosoever is convicted of theft shall have his head shaved, melted pitch poured upon it, and the feathers from a pillow be shaken over it, that he may be known; and shall be put on shore on the first land which the ship touches.'

He planned to winter in Sicily on the way to the Holy Land but, finding the Sicilians inhospitable, took Messina by force, making his nephew heir to the Sicilian throne by marrying him to the king's daughter. Richard also invaded Cyprus. Landing in Palestine with his ally Philip II of France on 8 June 1191, he joined the siege of Acre (now Akko in Israel) which, by then, had been underway for two years. Within six weeks, Richard had defeated the Muslim defenders, taken the city and put 2,700 prisoners to the sword.

Richard then welded the multinational crusaders into a single force. He marched them down the coast, where they could be supplied by ship. They travelled in battle order in three divisions of three columns, defended by crossbowmen from Saladin's horse-borne archers who harassed them.

On 7 September 1191 at Arsuf, Saladin attacked in force. Richard kept the crusaders on the defensive for most of the day, repelling attack after attack. Then when the Muslim forces were tiring, the Master of the Knights Hospitallers, commanding the rearguard, suddenly charged. Richard then ordered the whole crusader force to surge forward, taking the Muslim army by surprise. The rout was complete. Richard's force was so disciplined he stopped them chasing the fleeing Muslim soldiers, who tried to lure the crusaders into the desert. Some 7,000 of Saladin's men were killed at the loss of 700 crusaders.

As Saladin retreated towards Jerusalem, he left scorched earth behind him. Away from the coast and his ships, Richard could not supply his men and he was forced to abandon his ambition of taking Jerusalem. For the next year, skirmishing continued, then in September 1192 Saladin agreed to a three-year truce, which left Acre and a thin coastal strip in the crusaders' hands and gave Christians the right to visit the holy places in Jerusalem.

Richard headed home, but his ship was wrecked near Venice. He travelled overland in disguise but was captured near Vienna in December 1192 by a personal enemy, Duke Leopold of Austria, and eventually landed over to Heinrich VI, Holy Roman Emperor. The English people then had to raise an enormous ransom of 150,000 marks. Its collection was organized by Eleanor of Aquitaine. Richard also had to surrender his English kingdom and French territories, though Heinrich returned them to him as an imperial fiefdom. Meanwhile, his brother John tried to seize the throne with the aid of Philip II.

Richard was released in February 1194 and returned to England where he was crowned a second time. John was banished, though was later reconciled with his brother. Within a month Richard was back in Normandy, leaving England in the hands of Hubert Walter, his chief minister and Archbishop of Canterbury. In France Richard fought a prolonged campaign against Philip II. For five years, Richard fought Philip to hold on to the English possessions in France, which were eventually lost when his brother John succeeded him. As well as fighting across

Anjou, Maine, Touraine, Aquitaine and Gascony, Richard built major fortifications including the great fort at Château-Gaillard on an island in the River Seine. In 1199, while besieging the castle of the Archbishop of Limoges at Châlus, Richard was hit in the shoulder by an arrow from a crossbow. Gangrene set in and he died on 6 April, aged 41. Richard was buried in the abbey church at Fontevault, beside his parents Henry II and Eleanor of Aquitaine.

King John

Richard was succeeded by his brother John (1199–1216). He was Henry II's youngest son and his favourite. When he was betrothed to the daughter of Humbert III, count of Maurienne (Savoy), Henry proposed to give him extensive territories. But his brothers rebelled. John was then stuck with the nickname 'Lackland' and the marriage did not go ahead. However, provisions were made in England. In 1176, after the death of the earl of Gloucester, John was betrothed to his daughter Isabella on terms that disinherited her sisters and their husbands. And in 1177 he was given lordship of Ireland, which he visited in 1185.

When Richard took the throne, he made John count of Mortain in south-west Normandy. He was also confirmed as lord of Ireland. In England he was given Peverel, Lancaster, Marlborough and Ludgershall – with their castles – along with Tickhill, Wallingford and the counties of Derby and Nottingham – without their castles, which were held by the crown. He was also given Cornwall, Devon, Somerset, and Dorset, bringing him revenues of some £6,000 a year. When he finally married Isabella – in defiance of the Archbishop of Canterbury's prohibition on the grounds of consanguinity – he inherited her father's estates. In March 1190, Richard made him heir to the duchy of Normandy. In return, John had to promise that he would not enter England for three years while Richard was away on his crusade.

In October 1190, the childless Richard named his three-year-old nephew Arthur, duke of Brittany, the son of his deceased brother Geoffrey, heir to the throne of England. John immediately broke his promise, landed in England and forced Richard's chancellor to flee to France. When Philip II returned to France, he offered to help John take over the Angevin lands on the Continent, if he would marry his sister Alix, who Richard had previously been betrothed to.

Richard was then in prison in Austria. John spread the word in England that Richard was dead and demanded the allegiance of his subjects. But the lie did not convince. John's castles were besieged and preparations were made against an invasion by John's French allies. When the ransom demand came from Austria, John made a truce. Soon afterwards John received a message from Philip, saying: 'The Devil is loosed.' Assuming that Richard was about to be released and that he would soon be facing a charge of treason, John fled to France. Philip and John then offered a bribe to Richard's captors to keep him or hand him over to them.

When Richard was ransomed in 1194, John was banished and stripped of all his possessions. However, the following year, there was a reconciliation and some lands, including Mortain and Ireland, were returned to him. Then, in 1196, Philip II managed to capture Arthur of Brittany, who he brought up in his household. Richard disinherited him and recognized John as his heir.

On Richard's death, John was invested as duke of

Normandy and crowned king of England. But Arthur, backed by Philip II, was recognized as Richard's successor in Maine and Anjou. The following year, Philip II recognized John as the successor in all Richard's French possessions, in return for money and territorial concessions.

John had his marriage to Isabella annulled and married the heiress to Angoulême, who had been betrothed to Hugh IX de Lusignan. The Lusignans rebelled. Philip II intervened and war broke out. John captured Arthur at Mirebeau-en-Poitou. Arthur was imprisoned and, according to tradition, was murdered either by John or on his orders. But after that Normandy, Maine and Anjou were quickly lost.

John now spent most of his time in England. To pay for the war, he upped taxes – making a special tax on Jews – and enforced feudal prerogatives. John then fell out with the pope over his selection of the next Archbishop of Canterbury and was excommunicated. He got this lifted by paying a tribute of 1,000 marks (£666 13 shillings and 4 pence). However, he had succeeded in alienating England's churchmen, along with the barons – largely because he made free with their wives and daugthers. There was an unsuccessful plot to murder him during a campaign planned against the Welsh.

John launched one more campaign in France in 1214, but was forced to accept a truce. When he returned to England, the country was on the verge of rebellion. Despite lengthy negotiations, civil war broke out the following year and, when London turned against him, John was forced to come to terms. On 15 June 1215, he met his barons in a field at Runnymede. They brought with them a document containing their demands known as the Articles of the Barons. After revisions were made, the king and the barons signed what became known as Magna Carta.

However, John had no intention of living up to the provisions of Magna Carta. He immediately wrote to Pope Innocent III (1198–1216) asking him to annul the charter. Innocent excommunicated the barons. Civil war broke out again. The barons called for help from the French Prince Louis – later Louis VIII (1223–6), also known as Louis *le Lion* or Louis *Coeur-de-lion* – who invaded. John fought on until he died in 1216, leaving the problem to be resolved by his nine-year-old son who succeeded as Henry III (1216–72).

King John's heirs

Under Henry, the antagonism between the Normans and Saxons should have subsided as Henry III was the first Plantagenet to be born in England and spend most of his life there. However, the barons objected to the favouritism he showed his foreign friends in court. And when he got himself involved in a series of costly wars, they demanded a say in the selection of the King's counsellors. He finally conceded this in 1258, but in 1264 Simon de Montfort rebelled.

When de Monfort was defeated at the battle of Evesham in August 1265, Henry's son Edward took charge of government, before ruling in his own right as Edward I (1272–1307). The first part of his reign was dominated by his campaigns in Wales, finally bringing the province under the English legal and administrative system. He invaded Scotland in 1296. Opposition gathered around Sir William Wallace but he was captured by the English and brought to London where he was executed in 1305.

Edward I was succeeded by Edward II (1307–27). His reign was marred by a number of allegedly homosexual relationships that earned the opprobrium of the barons. In 1314, Edward attempted to emulate his father and invaded Scotland, only to be decisively defeated by Robert the Bruce at Bannockburn. His weakness and his scandalous behaviour led to the short-lived rebellion of Thomas, earl of Lancaster, in 1322 – a key event in one of the historical interpretations of the Robin Hood story.

13

ROBIN HOOD IN HOLLYWOOD

With the American success of Howard Pyle's *The Adventures of Robin Hood* and Arthur Sullivan's *The Foresters: Robin Hood and Maid Marian*, the English action hero was all set to conquer the silver screen when the movies moved to Hollywood in the early years of the twentieth century. However, the first Robin Hood movie, *Robin Hood and His Merry Men*, directed by Percy Stow, was made in England in 1908.

In 1912, a 30-minute silent film called simply *Robin Hood* was shot in Fort Lee, New Jersey, starring Robert Frazier. The following year Robin also turned up in *Ivanhoe*, filmed in Wales by the American Independent Moving Pictures Company, while another *Robin Hood* was made in America. The silent classic *Robin Hood* was made in 1922. It starred Douglas Fairbanks, who had already established himself at the swashbuckling king of Hollywood with *Mark of Zorro* in 1920 and *The Three Musketeers* in 1921. This was the first Robin Hood movie to be made in California. It set the action in the late twelfth century during the time Richard is at the crusades and John is trying to take his throne, a period it has occupied ever since. Robin is the dispossessed Earl of Huntingdon, who fights his arch-enemy Sir Guy of Gisborne. The Japanese made a version called *Robin Hood no yume* in 1924, while Will Rogers did a spoof of the Fairbanks' movie in the short *Big Moments from Little Pictures*.

By 1938, Robin could talk – and appear in colour – in *The Adventures of Robin Hood*, starring Errol Flynn. Although this was Flynn's most acclaimed role, it did not win him an Oscar. However, the film did win Oscars for Best Art Direction, Best Film Editing and Best Original Score, and was nominated for Best Picture. It used some of the same locations as the 1922 production. Again it was set during John's usurpation with Robin as the dis-possessed Saxon Earl of Locksley. King Richard returns disguised as a monk. Robin prevents John taking the throne after a prolonged sword fight during his coronation. Richard then reveals himself, exiles John and restores Robin's earldom so he can marry Maid Marian.

The short *The Merry Men of Sherwood* was made in the UK in 1932 and there was another British version of *Robin Hood* in 1935. In 1941 came *Robin Hood of the Pecos*, starring the 'Singing Cowboy' Roy Rogers, which moved the action to Texas after the Civil War. Then, in 1947, there was *Robin Hood of Texas* with Gene Autry, playing himself, pitted against a gang of bank robbers.

In 1946 Robin Hood returned to medieval England – on screen at least – with *The Bandit of Sherwood Forest*. It carried the tagline: 'The Son of Robin Hood'. Cornel Wilde starred as, variously, Robert of Nottingham and Robert of Huntington, while Russell Hicks played his father, Robin Hood. *The Prince of Thieves* – the 'revealing new daring adventures of Robin Hood' – followed in 1948. Then came *Rogues of Sherwood Forest* starring John Derek as Robin Hood and Alan Hale, Sr, as Little John, a role he had played opposite Douglas Fairbanks in 1922 and Errol Flynn in 1938.

In 1951, the Merry Men were pitted against the Sheriff of Nottingham in *Tales of Robin Hood*. The following year Disney shot *The Story of Robin Hood and His Merrie Men*, starring Richard Todd, in Buckinghamshire. Robin's father is killed by Prince John's henchmen and Robin takes to the forest to avenge him and protect the populace from the Sheriff's tax gatherers. The British responded with *Miss Robin Hood* about the author of a comic strip whose heroine robs banks with the assistance of a gang of teenage girls, then distributes the proceeds. When the comic strip is dropped, the author is encouraged to emulate the heroine's crimes. That same year, Robin appeared again in *Ivanhoe*, starring Robert Taylor, Elizabeth Taylor, Joan Fontaine and George Sanders. The Disney animated version of *Robin Hood* came out in 1973.

The BBC began producing the TV series *Robin Hood*, starring Patrick Troughton, in 1953. With the advent of a commercial TV channel in the UK in 1955, a new series called *The Adventures of Robin Hood* started. It starred Richard Greene and ran until 1960 in the UK and 1959 on CBS in the US. The series was made by Sapphire

Films, which was set up by Hannah Weinstein, a member of the Hollywood branch of the Communist Party. After the House Un-American Activities Committee began its blacklist of suspected Communists working in Hollywood, the Communist Party sent Weinstein to London with the money to sent up the company. She used blacklisted writers including Ring Lardner Jr and his writing partner Ian McClellan Hunter to produce the first series, which was aired in the UK and syndicated in America. On the second series, more blacklisted writers were brought in. They wrote under pseudonyms and Weinstein went to great lengths to prevent the American authorities discovering who her writers were. Living in London, she was beyond the HUAC's reach.

However, by the late 1950s, the power of the HUAC began to decline. In 1959, former President Harry S. Truman denounced the committee as 'the most un-American thing in the country today'. When the blacklist broke down, Lardner remarked that the format of the Robin Hood series had afforded him 'plenty of opportunities to comment on issues and institutions in Eisenhower-era America'. As well as being sympathetic to the Communist ideal of taking from the rich to give to the poor, many episodes showed Robin and his men being betrayed to the authorities, a theme all too familiar to the blacklisted writers.

Robin quickly became a stock character for sketch shows and Warner Bros cast Daffy Duck as Robin in a six-minute cartoon in 1958. While many more movies and TV series about Robin Hood were made in English, the Merry Men began to move out into the world. In 1956, a TV series named *Robin Hood* was being made in Brazil. *Robin Hood e i pirati* appeared in Italy in 1960 – on the way home from the crusades, Robin is shipwrecked and saved by pirates. After being shipwrecked again and washed ashore in England, they join forces with him. *Robin Hood en zijn schelmen* appeared in the Netherlands in 1962, while *Il trionfo de Robin Hood* took Robin back to Italy.

In 1964 *Robin and the Seven Hoods* set the story in prohibition-era Chicago and starred Frank Sinatra and the Rat Pack. Two years later, *Robin Hood, de edle Ritter* took Robin to West Germany. In 1969, *The Ribald Tales of Robin Hood* turned the action in Sherwood Forest into erotica. A Swedish company made the Spanish *Las nuevas aventures de Robin de los Bosques*, which appeared in Italy as *Il magnifico Robin Hood* in 1970. It was competing with *L'arciere di Sherwood*, which was also shown in Spain, France and Finland. The Finns also produced a TV version in 1972 called simply *Robin Hood*.

The Brazilians made a comedy version in 1974 called *Robin Hood, O Trapalhão da Floresta*. That year, the Finns produced another TV version called *Robin Hood ja hänen iloiset vekkulinsa Sherwoodin pusikoissa*. Then, in 1975, the Russians produced their version, *Strely Robin Guda*.

Mel Brooks first got in on the act in 1975 with the TV series *When Things Were Rotten*. His *Robin Hood: Men in Tights* appeared in 1993. Meanwhile, Finland, Italy, Spain, West Germany and Brazil had another fix with *Storia di arcieri, pugni e occhi neri* in 1976. That year, *Robin and Marian* took a more mature look at the legend. An ageing Robin Hood, played by Sean Connery, returns from the crusades to find Maid Marian, played by Audrey Hepburn, in a convent. Yet again he has to rescue her from his life-long enemy the Sheriff of Nottingham, before Robin and Marian once again become lovers.

In 1983, Robin Hood turned up in the Russian version of *Ivanhoe: Ballada o doblestnom rytsare Ayvengo*. That year, *Robin Hood and the Sorcerer* played in the Philippines. In 1990, the Japanese produced the animated series *Robin Hood no Dai Boken*, where the Merry Men are children. Between 1989 and 1994, the British TV show *Maid Marian and her Merry Men* made Marian the dynamic leader of the resistance against Prince John. Kevin Costner brought back a full Hollywood production in 1991 with *Robin Hood: Prince of Thieves*, though it was shot largely in England and France. The French joined forces with the Turner Network in 1997 to produce *The New Adventures of Robin Hood* that put Robin in black leather. It was filmed in Lithuania. The Germans produced *Drei für Robin Hood* in 2003, while *Keloglan kara prens'e karsi* came out in Turkey in 2006.

Since the character of Robin Hood is in the public domain, there is no restriction on his use. He has appeared as a minor character in numerous films, plays, books, cartoons and TV shows. There also seems to be an endless appetite worldwide for the reworking of the legend of Robin Hood. Now, in 2010, Russell Crowe and Ridley Scott are adding new dimensions to the myth.

CHRONOLOGY

1066	Norman invasion of England by William the Conqueror.
1070–71	Hereward the Wake's resistance to the Norman invasion.
1100–25	*Gesta Herewardi* written.
1154	The first mention of Sherwood Forest by name.
1160	Birth of Robin Hood, according to John Major.
1170	Birth of Fulk FitzWarin and Eustace the Monk.
1189	Accession of Richard I.
1193	Philip Augustus of France invades English-ruled Normandy.
1193–4	Richard I held captive in Germany.
1196	Robert Fitz Odo loses his estates in Loxley.
1197	Fulk FitzWarin becomes lord of Whittington.
1199	Death of Richard I. Accession of King John.
1200	Fulk FitzWarin outlawed on charges of treason.
1203	Fulk FitzWarin pardoned by King John. The *Feet of Fines* records Robert Fitz Odo in Harbury.
1204	Eustace the Monk becomes an outlaw.

1213–16	A Robert Hood commits murder at Cirencester Abbey.
1215	Fulk FitzWarin joins the baron's revolt. King John signs Magna Carta at Runnymede.
1216	Death of King John. Accession of Henry III.
1217	Fulk FitzWarin makes peace with Henry III. Death of Eustace the Monk.
1223–84	*Li romans de Witass le Moine* records the life of Eustace the Monk.
1224	Franciscan friars arrive in England.
1225	Robert Hod of York recorded as a fugitive.
1226	'Hobbehod' outlaw in Yorkshire.
1247	Death of Robin Hood, according to Thomas Gale and Joseph Ritson.
1258	Death of Fulk FitzWarin.
1260	Probable date for the composition of the *Fouke le Fitz Waryn*.
1262	William Robehod, son of Robert le Fevre, outlawed in Berkshire.
1264	Henry III defeated by Simon de Montfort, earl of Leicester. Death of FitzWarin's son at the battle of Lewes.
1265	Henry's son, Prince Edward, defeats Simon de Montfort at Evesham.
1266	Robin Hood's first confrontation with the 'viscount' or sheriff, according to Walter Bower. Sheriff William de Grey wages war on the outlaws in Sherwood Forest.
1272	Death of Henry III. Accession of Edward I on his return from Palestine.
1283	The French poet Adam de la Halle writes pastoral poem, *Le Jeu de Robin et Marion*.
1283–5	Scottish historian Andrew Wyntoun places Little John and Robin Hood in Inglewood and Barnsdale.

1287	William Scathlock is recorded as a monk at St Mary's Abbey in York.
1295	Henry de Faucumberg inherits his father's estates in Yorkshire.
1296	Scotland defeated by Edward I. First appearance of surname 'Robynhod' with Gilbert Robynhod in Fletching, Sussex.
1297–1305	William Wallace's resistance to English rule in Scotland.
1301	A deed pertaining to the manor of Hornington, eight miles south-west of York, describes Roger of Doncaster as a chaplain.
1304	Robin Hood named in the *Registrum Premonstratense*.
1306	The Scottish bishops taken south to Winchester as prisoners require extra armed guards as they travel through Barnsdale. Roger of Doncaster is sent by the Archbishop of York to be priest at Ruddington church, near Nottingham.
1307	Death of Edward I. Succession of Edward II. Alice de Scriven becomes Prioress of Kirklees.
1309	'Sir Roger of Doncaster' is charged with adultery with one Agnes, the wife of a Philip de Pavely.
1313	Henry de Faucumberg is fined for stealing wood from the barn of Lord Warenne in Wakefield.
1314	Edward II is defeated by Robert the Bruce at Bannockburn. Henry de Faucumberg is again fined for stealing wood in Wakefield. A Matilda de Toothill is also fined for collecting firewood without permission.
1315	Henry de Faucumberg refuses to take an oath and suffers a further fine for theft in Wakefield. The Archbishop of York hears scandalous reports about the nuns of Kirklees.

1316   Robert and Matilda Hood of Wakefield buy a plot of
            land at Bichill.

1317   A court held in Rasterick records that a 'Richard of the
            Lee dues William of the Watirhouse'.

1318   Henry de Faucumberg becomes Sheriff of Notting-
            ham. Robert Hood of Wakefield is included in a
            summons to fight in the army against the Scots. He
            fails to appear and is fined three pence.

1322   The Lancastrian revolt. Robert Hood of Wakefield is
            summoned to fight for the earl of Lancaster in his
            rebellion against the King. No fine is imposed for non-
            attendance.

1323   Edward II's royal progress reaches Nottingham in
            November. The day-book of the royal chamber
            records a Robyn Hode receiving wages on 27 June for
            the period 5–14 June.

1323–5   Henry de Faucumberg's second term as Sheriff of
            Nottingham.

1324   Between 24 March and 22 November, a Robyn Hode
            is employed as a royal *valet de chambre*. Joseph
            Hunter compared this record to events late in the *Gest*.
            Henry de Faucumberg appointed commissioner for
            Derbyshire, Staffordshire and Shropshire, to repossess
            Contrariants' lands.

1325   Henry de Faucumberg becomes keeper of Nottingham
            Castle. Robin Hood's return to Barnsdale, according
            to Joseph Hunter. Katherine Robynhod (possible
            patronymic) in London Coroner's roll.

1325–7   Henry de Faucumberg becomes Sheriff of Yorkshire.

1326   Henry de Faucumberg instructed to track down an
            outlaw gang led by Eustace de Folville.

1327   Isabella deposes Edward II. Edward III crowned king.
            Death of Edward II. A court held at Wakefield orders

eight acres of land at Criggleston to be given to a Roger, son of William of Doncaster.

1328	Roger of Doncaster again mentioned as vicar of Ruddington.
1328–30	Henry de Faucumberg's second term as Sheriff of Yorkshire.
1331	Elizabeth de Staynton becomes Prioress of Kirklees.
1332	Robert Robynhod recorded in West Harting, Sussex.
1333	Roger of Doncaster is imprisoned at Nottingham for trespassing in Sherwood Forest.
1347	The probable date for the death of Robin Hood of the *Gest*. Death of Elizabeth de Staynton, Prioress of Kirklees.
1348	Margaret de Savile becomes the Prioress of Kirklees. Black Death arrives in England.
1350	*The Tale of Gamelyn* appears.
1354	A man named Robin Hood awaiting trial in prison for offences in Rockingham forest.
1377	William Langland's *Piers Plowman*, mentions 'Robin Hood rhymes'.
1380	John Gower mentions Robin and Marion in *Mirour de l'homme*.
*c.*1380	Geoffrey Chaucer mentions Robyn in *Troilus and Criseyde*.
1381	Priest John Ball tells the rebels of the Peasants' Revolt to 'chastise wel Hobbe the Robbere'. Robert Robynhod, Winchelsea, recorded at Sussex.
1392	Adam de la Halle's *Robin and Marion* begins annual performances at Angers at Whitsuntide.
1400	Putative date for the composition of the *Gest*.
*c.*1400–25	Manuscript in Lincoln Cathedral mentions 'Robin Hood in Scherewood stod'.
*c.*1405–10	The Franciscan author of the religious discourse, *Dives*

and Pauper, castigates those who would rather 'hear a tale or a song of Robin Hood . . . than to hear Mass or Matins'. Hugh Legat preaches sermon, saying: 'For mani, manime seith, spekith of Robin Hood that schotte never in his bowe'.

1417   A royal writ of 1417 refers to renegade Sussex priest Robert Stafford, the chaplain of Lindfield, who has assumed the name 'Friar Tuck'.

1419–20   Poem *Reply of Friar Daw Topias* repeats Legat proverb: 'And many men speken of Robyn Hood and shotte nevere in his bowe'.

1420   Andrew de Wyntoun, in his *Original Chronicle of Scotland*, talks of the renowned outlaws Little John and Robin Hood in Inglewood and Barnsdale in the early 1280s. He also refers to one 'Hwde of Edname' who helped Alexander Ramsay take Roxburgh in 1342, possibly another reference to a Robin Hood.

1422   A deed from Yorkshire's Monk Bretton Priory mentions a Robin Hood's Stone, marking a field boundary near Slephill a mile to the south of Barnsdale Bar.

*c.*1425   Marginal note in manuscript of *Troilus and Criseyde* mentions Robin Hood.

1426–7   Earliest reference to Robin Hood plays in Exeter, ten years after first reference to May play there.

1429   A letter refers to Robert Stafford of Sussex as Friar Tuck. Lawsuit in Court of Common pleas makes first mention of legal formula 'Robin Hode in Barnsdale stode'.

1432   Parliament Roll for Wiltshire includes humorous addition of 'Adam Belle, Clym O'Cluw, Willyam Cloudesle . . . Robyn Hode, Lytel Joon, Muchette Millerson, Scathelok, Reynoldyn'.

1438	Ship called *Robyn Hude* or *ly Robert Hude* at Aberdeen.
1439	Piers Venables, 'gentilman' of Aston Derby, and his followers compared to 'Robyn Hobe and his meyne' in a petition to parliament.
1441	A group of yeomen and labourers block the road in Southacre, Norfolk, singing 'We are Robynhodesmen, war war war', and threatening to murder Sir Geoffrey Harsyk.
c.1441	Writing in the *Scotichronicon*, Walter Bower assigns Robin Hood to 1266 and describes Robin's first confrontation with the 'viscount' or sheriff in the forest.
1450	Surviving copy of *Robin Hood and the Monk* composed. *Robyn and Gandelyn* is composed.
1460–80	In the Physician's College manuscript of *The Canterbury Tales*, the tale of Sir Thopas, Robin Hood is substituted for Bevis of Hampton and mentions 'Robynhoode and sir Gy'.
1473	Sir John Paston of Norfolk, in a letter to his brother, writes how he had paid a servant to act in plays of Robin Hood. He also refers to Barnsdale as Robin's base.
1474	Money gathered by Robin Hod play in Thame, Oxfordshire.
1475	The *Dramatic Fragment* includes a few lines from *Robin Hood and Guy of Gisborne*. References to Robin Hood in village plays in Croscombe, North Somerset, begin. *A Gest of Robyn Hode* appears.
1485	First known reference to a landmark in Nottingham bearing the name of Robin Hood – Robin Hood Close.
1486	Henry VII meets the earl of Northumberland near Robin Hood's Stone in Barnsdale.
1487–8	Robin Hood plays in Exeter.

1492 Robettus Hod in Edinburgh May games.

1496 More money gathered by Robin Hood play in Thame, Oxfordshire.

1498 Roger Marshall of Wednesbury in Staffordshire uses the name Robin Hood in a riot in nearby Willenhall.

c.1498 'Tempus de Robynhode' plays at Wells, Somerset.

1498–9 'Gaderyngs of Robin Hood' at Reading.

1499 Henley-on-Thames council resolves that money collected at Robin Hood game be spent on silver censer.

Late 15th century Robin Hood and his men mentioned in 'Men of Cumberland' poem. Ironic reference of 'Robyn Hode' in *How the Plowman Learned his Pater Noster*, also mentioned in Scottish, Porkington and Lambeth manuscripts.

c.1500 Welsh song '*Robin Hwd ai kant*' in manuscript.

1500 A Robin Hood's Well is recorded in Nottingham. Little John joins Robin Hood in Edinburgh May games. *Robin Hood and the Potter* published.

1500–10 Anonymous Scottish poem mentions 'Johne nor Robene Hude' alongside 'Wallace'.

1501 More money gathered by Robin Hood play at Thame, Oxfordshire. Mention of Robin Hood in Gavin Douglas's *Palace of Honour*.

1501–3 Mention of Robyn Hude in *Ane Littill Interlud of the Droichis Part of the Play* formally attributed to William Dunbar.

1502 The surviving copy of *Robin Hood and the Potter* is written on the back of a document detailing the expenses for the feast of the marriage of Henry VII's daughter, Princess Margaret, to James IV of Scotland.

1503 King of Scotland plays Robin Hood of Perth.

1503–8 William Dunbar's poem *Of Sir Thomas Norray* mentions 'Robeine', 'Gy of Gysburne' and Allan Bell.

1505	Robin Hood of Finchamstead and 'Hendley' (Henley-on-Thames) visit Reading.
1506–7	Beginning of costume records for Robin Hood. The 'frere', the lady and Little John associated with Morris dancing at Kingston-on-Thames.
1507	Last appearance of Robin Hood at Reading.
1508	Alexander Barclay's, *The Ship of Follies*, includes the oldest surviving reference to Maid Marian along with three references to Robin Hood. Little John and Robin Hood appear at May games at Aberdeen later that year on St Nicholas's day. St John's, Exeter, pay for renovation of St Edmund's arrow for Robin Hood.
1509	Maid Marian named for first time at Kingston.
1509–10	Robin Hood plays banned in Exeter as a public nuisance.
1510	*A Geste of Robyn Hode* is published. Eleven nobles break into the Queen's chamber, dressed as Robin Hood and his Merry Men.
1512–25	Household accounts of Henry Percy, fifth earl of Northumberland, put aside to buy livery of Robin Hood at his two Yorkshire castles.
1513	Tinrinhull, Somerset, produce Robin Hood's ale.
1515	Henry VIII guest of Robin Hood at May festival. A second edition of the *Gest*, entitled *A Lytlell Geste of Robyn Hode*, is published by the English printer Wynken de Worde.
1517–18	Robin Hood and Little John in May games in Aberdeen.
1518	Impersonation of Robin Hood and Little John by tenants of Prior of Worcester begins.
c.1520	In catalogue of Oxford bookseller 'Roban Hood' price tuppence.

1520   John Rastell *Interlude of Four Elements* includes song
             beginning 'Robin Hood in Barnesdale stood'. Robin
             Hood's money appears in Henley-on-Thames Parish
             register. John Skelton's play *Magnificence* mentions
             Friar Tuck.

1521   Scottish writer John Major, in his *History of Greater
             Britain*, states that Robin was outlawed between 1193
             and 1194 while Richard I was held captive in Germany.
             Robin Hood play at May games in Dundee.

1526–7   Robin Hood play in Ashburton, Devon, involving the
             purchase of a new tunic made for Robin Hood.

1528   Robin Hood play in Worcester. In *The Obedience of a
             Christian Man*, William Tyndale condemns tales of
             Robin Hood and other 'fables of love and wantoness,
             and ribaldry' that 'corrupt the minds of youth'.

1529   In *A Dialogue Concerning Heresies* Sir Thomas More
             says: 'To handle holie scripture is more homely maner
             than a song of Robin Hood.'

1530   Henry VIII paid for twelve actors to take part in a
             Robin Hood dance. Money received 'of the lord for
             Robin Hood' in Amersham. Tenants play with Robin
             Hood and Maid Marian in late July at Cleeve Prior,
             Worcestershire.

1531   The Lord High Treasurer of Scotland mentions 'taffaris of
             Jeynes to be ane part of the Kingis Robin Hood baner'.

1532   Robin Hood play in Hythe, Kent.

1533   Thomas More mentions the tale of Robin Hood again
             in *The Confutation of Tyndale's Answer*.

1534   Robin Hood and Little John appear at May games in
             Dumfries. In Leicester, church officials complain about
             Robin Hood games. Robert Fabyan's *Chronicle*,
             published 1534, notes: 'many of Robin Hodes pagentes,
             which named himself Granelef'.

1535	Robin Hood plays begin at Ombersley, Worcestershire.
1536	Window at Betley, Staffordshire, showing Maid Marian and Friar Tuck. Robin Hood plays begin at Stratton, Cornwall.
1536–7	Robin Hood plays at Dumfries.
c.1536–9	Sir Richard Morison urges Henry VIII to ban the Robin Hood plays as subversive.
1537	Play *Thersites* mentions 'Robin John and Little Hood' along with Friar Tuck.
1538	Last reference to Robin Hood at Kingston-on-Thames.
1539–40	Robin Hood plays at Ayr in May.
1540	Robin Hood Stone recorded in Whitby, Yorkshire.
1540–41	Coats were bought for Robin Hood and Little John at Woodbury, Devon.
1541–2	Tunic bought for Robin Hood play in Ashburton, Devon.
1542	John Leland, Henry VIII's chief antiquarian, refers to Robin Hood as a nobleman in his *Collectanea* and associates him with Barnsdale and Kirklees. Nicholas Udall's *Apothegmes* mentions the tales of Robin Hood and Barnsdale.
1542–3	Robin Hood play in Ayr.
1543	End of Robin Hood plays in Stratton, Cornwall.
1544	Robin Hood's Bay recorded in Yorkshire.
1545	Robin Hood at May games in Perth. William Turner in *The Rescuing of the Romish Fox* charges Bishop Gardiner with forbidding plays about Christ, while encouraging those about Robin Hood and Little John.
1546–51	More Robin Hood plays in Ayr.
1548	Robin Hood walk in Richmond Park, Surrey begun.
1549	Wedderburn's *Complaint of Scotland* refers to Robin

Hood tales and dances. Bishop Latimer attacks Robin Hood games and those who 'prefer Robin Hood to God's word'.

1550   Latimer renews attack on Robin Hood in sermon before Edward VI. Putative dates of the ballads *Robin Hood and the Curtal Friar* and *Robin Hood and the Butcher*.

1553   Robin Hood play at Shrewsbury. Robin Hood May games mentioned in Richard Robinson's *Ancient Order of Prince Arthur*.

1553–4 Robin Hood ale appears in Exeter. A Robin Hood play involving gunpowder put on in Ayr.

1553–8 *A Tale of Robin Hood or The Overthrowe of the Abbyes* – an allegory of the dissolution of the monasteries, with Robin Hood representing the bishops, Adam Bell the abbots and Little John the universities.

1554–5 First reference to Robin Hood plays in Chagford, Devon, where young men of the parish are paid for the 'howde'.

1555   Robin Hood appears at May games in Peebles. Scottish parliament bans Robin Hood and Little John from May games.

1556   A churchwarden of St Helen's in Abingdon, Berkshire, mentions the setting up of a 'Robin Hood's Bower'. Money collected at Robin Hood plays in Melton Mowbray, Leicestershire.

1557–8 Ballad *Of Wakefylde and a Grene* – probably *Robin Hood and the Pinder* – appears in Stationer's Register. More hoods bought for Robin Hood play in Chagford, Devon.

1559   Robin Hood, Little John, Maid Marian and Friar Tuck appear at May games around London. Queen attends games in Greenwich.

1559–60   Hoodsmen paid at Chagford.

1560–61   St Brannock's Church pays for meat and drink for Robin Hood plus company in Braunton, Devon.

1561   Edinburgh riots after the 'maner of Robin Hood', according to John Knox. Money paid out for costume for Robin Hood and players in Chudleigh, Devon; later money paid from the games into church coffers.

1561–2   St Brannock's Church buys cloth for Robin Hood's coat, and at Whitsun pays the company.

1562   Publication of Richard Grafton's *Chronicle* which claimed to have discovered an 'olde and aunciente Pamphlet' recording Robin's life as a lord, along with 'records in the Exchequer rolls' referring to the confiscation of his lands; he assigns Robin to the reign of Richard I. Mary Queen of Scots confirms ban on Robin Hood.

1562–3   *Ballett of Robin Hood* appears in Stationer's Register.

1563–4   Hoodsmen in Chagford are paid again and St Brannock's in Braunton buys Little John a coat.

1565   Illegal Robin Hood games held in Aberdeen. Minstrel Sandy Stevin convicted of blasphemy on the grounds 'that he believed as well a tale of Robin Hood as any word written in the Old Testament or New'.

1566   A Robin Hood play performed in Abingdon, Berkshire.

1570   Robin Hood play in Dumfries. But in Arburthnott, Scotland, the selection of a Robin Hood leads to a treason charge.

1571   Honiton buys a pound of gunpowder when Robin Hood of Colyton comes to town.

1573–4   A Robin Hood gathering was held at Woodbury,

Devon. Twenty-five yards of canvas were bought to make Robin Hood's 'house'.

1575 Hector Bocce makes reference to Little John in his *Scotorum Historiae a Prima Gentis Origine*, claiming to have seen his enormous bones in Moray. Morris dance at Kenilworth includes Maid Marian.

1576–7 Honiton pays Robin Hood. Robin Hood ale produced in Woodbury, Devon.

1577 Scottish General Assembly requests prohibition of Robin Hood plays on the sabbath. They are condemned by Laurence Ramsay in *The practice of the Diuell.*

1578 Robin Hood replace by 'Keeper of the Ale' in Yeovil.

1579 Proclamation against Robin Hood plays in Edinburgh.

1581–2 Two green coats bought for Robin Hood and Little John in Woodbury, Devon.

1582 Christopher Fetherstone's *Dialogue Agaynst light,* 'lewde, and lasciuious dancing' condemns 'may-marrions'; men must not put on women's apparel.

1582–3 Robin Hood appears at May games in Dalkeith.

1584 Robin Hood play at St Ives, Cornwall. Richard Wilson's play *The Three Ladies of London* condemns telling tales of Robin Hood on the Sabbath.

1585 At Dirleton, the King of Scotland 'passed the time with the play of Robin Hood'.

1588 Robin Hood plays prohibited in Haddington, Scotland. Performed at St Columb Major and St Columb Minor, Cornwall, and Bridgenorth, Shropshire. Last referencc to Robin Hood play in Chagford; Hoodsmen keep the silver arrow.

1590 Robin Hood appears in May games in Cranston, Scotland.

1591 Scottish General Assembly again condemns Robin Hood plays.

1592	John Stow *Annales of England* assigns Robin Hood to period of Richard I, using Major as source.
1592–3	Shakespeare's *Two Gentlemen of Verona* mentions 'the bare scalp of Robin Hood's fat friar'.
1597	In Shakespeare's *Henry IV* Falstaff tells Mistress Quickly that 'Maid Marian may be the deputy's wife of the ward to thee', while Justice Silence sings the refrain 'Robin Hood, Scarlet and John' from *Robyn Hood and the Pindar of Wakefield*.
1598	Elizabethan playwright, Anthony Munday, writes *The Downfall of Robert, Earl of Huntington*. Robin Hood's Buttes is recorded near Brampton in Scotland.
1599	With Henry Chettle, Anthony Munday completes *The Death of Robert, Earl of Huntington*.
*c.*1600	Shakespeare's *As You Like It* refers to Robin Hood.
1600	*A Short Life of Robin Hood*, also known as the Sloan Manuscript, is compiled. *Looke About You*, a play featuring Robin Hood, earl of Huntington, who is involved with Marian, wife of Lord Fauconbridge.
1607	William Camden's *Britannia* mentions Robin Hood's grave in Kirklees.
1632	Martin Parker's *The True Tale of Robin Hood* is published.
1650	The Percy Folio is compiled, including two early Robin Hood ballads: *Robin Hood and Guy of Gisborne* and *Robin Hood and the Curtal Friar*.
1665	Pontefract antiquarian, Nathaniel Johnston, makes a drawing of Robin Hood's grave at Kirklees.
1680	Oldest surviving reference to Little John's grave at Hathersage, by antiquarian Elias Ashmole.
1700	In his *Travels over England*, diarist James Brame describes a Robin Hood society initiation ceremony at

St Anne's Well in Nottingham. The first recorded Sherwood landmark appears: Robin Hood's Cave near Rainworth.

1702   Reference found by Thomas Gale, the Dean of York, to the earl of Huntington in the epitaph on Robin Hood's grave at Kirklees.

1706   The gravestone of Elizabeth de Staynton is discovered at Kirklees Priory.

1729   Little John's bow is taken to Cannon Hall near Barnsley.

1730   Thomas Gent, in his *History of York*, records Robin Hood's Well in Barnsdale as 'a very handsome stone arch, erected by the earl of Carlisle, where passengers from the coach frequently drink'.

1746   William Stukeley constructs a genealogy which includes a Robert Fitz Othe as the earl of Huntington during the reign of Richard I.

1765   Thomas Percy, bishop of Dronmore in Ireland, discovers Robin Hood ballads in a mid-seventeenth-century manuscript in a Shropshire house and publishes them in his *Reliques of Ancient English Poetry*.

1784   Reverend Charles Spencer Stanhope mentions the large thigh bone from Little John's grave at Hathersage.

1785   An illustration of Elizabeth de Staynton's grave slab appears in a revised edition of William Camden's *Britannia*.

1789   Richard Gough's *Sepulchral Monuments of Great Britain* includes Nathaniel Johnston's drawing of the Kirklees grave.

1795   Joseph Ritson publishes a collection of ballads in his *Robin Hood*, subtitled 'A collection of all the ancient poems, songs and ballads now extant relating to that celebrated outlaw'. His introduction is called 'The Life of Robin Hood'.

1818	John Keats writes the poem *Robin Hood*.
1819	Robin Hood appears in Sir Walter Scott's *Ivanhoe*.
1840	Sir George Armytage of Kirklees Hall erects a new monument at Robin Hood's grave. Pierce Egan writes *Robin Hood & Little John* for children.
1846	Antiquarian Thomas Wright argues in his *Essays on the Literature of the Middle Ages* that Robin Hood was an imported Saxon myth.
1852	Joseph Hunter publishes *Mr Hunter's Critical and Historical Tracts. No IV: The Ballad Hero Robin Hood*, subtitled 'Robin Hood: His Period, Real Character, Etc. Investigated and Perhaps Ascertained'.
1864	J.R. Planche publishes his paper *A Ramble with Robin Hood*, suggesting that Robert Fitz Odo of Loxley in Warwickshire is Robin Hood.
1883	Howard Pyle publishes his *The Merry Adventures of Robin Hood of Great Renown in Nottinghamshire*.
1892	Alfred, Lord Tennyson and Arthur Sullivan's *The Foresters: Robin Hood and Maid Marian* goes on stage in New York.
1922	Silent classic *Robin Hood* starring Douglas Fairbanks made.
1929	Ancient Order of Foresters repairs Little John's grave at Hathersage.
1933	In *The God of the Witches*, Egyptologist Margaret Murray claims that Robin Hood had been a mythological figure in the European witch cult.
1938	Warner Bros make *The Adventures of Robin Hood* starring Errol Flynn.
1944	President of the Yorkshire Archaeological Society, J.W. Walker, publishes further evidence that Robert

Hood of Wakefield fought in the earl of Lancaster's army.

1951   Little John's bow removed from Cannon Hall and given to Wakefield Museum.

1991   *Robin Hood: Prince of Thieves* starring Kevin Costner.

2010   *Robin Hood* starring Russell Crowe.

BIBLIOGRAPHY

Bellamy, John (1985) *Robin Hood: An Historical Enquiry*, London: Croom Helm

Coghlan, Ronan (2003) *The Robin Hood Companion*, Bangor, County Down: Xiphos Books

Dobson, R.B. and Taylor, J. (1976) *Rymes of Robyn Hood: An Introduction to the English Outlaw*, Stroud: Sutton Publishing

Green, Barbara (2001) *Secrets of the Grave: The Story of the Fight to Save the Tomb of Robin Hood*, Brighouse: Palmyra Press

Hamilton of Gilbertfield, William (1998) *Blind Harry's Wallace*, Edinburgh: Luath Press

Harris, P. Valentine (1951) *The Truth About Robin Hood: A Refutation of the Mythologists' Theories, With New Evidence of the Hero's Actual Existence*, London: self-published

Hern, Thomas (ed.) (2000) *Robin Hood in Popular Culture*, Woodbridge: Boyell & Brewer, Woodbridge

Hobsbawm, Eric (2000) *Bandits*, London: Weidenfeld & Nicholson

Holt, J.C. (1982) *Robin Hood*, London: Thames & Hudson, 1982

Hunter, Joseph (1883) *The Great Hero of the Ancient Minstrelsy of England 'Robin Hood': His Period, Real Character, etc., Investigated and Perhaps Ascertained*, Worksop: Robert White

Knight, Stephen (1994) *Robin Hood: A Complete Study of the English Outlaw*, Oxford: Blackwell Publishers

— (2003) *Robin Hood: A Mythic Biography*, Ithaca, NY: Cornell University Press

— and Ohlgren, Thomas (eds) (2000) *Robin Hood and Other Outlaw Tales*, Kalamazoo, MI: Medieval Institute Publications, Western Michigan University

Lees, Jim (1987) *The Quest for Robin Hood*, Nottingham: Temple

Philips, Graham and Keatman, Martin (1995) *Robin Hood: The Man Behind the Myth,* London: Michael O'Mara Books

Phillips, Helen (ed.) (2005) *Robin Hood: Medieval and Post-Medieval*, Dublin: Four Courts Press

Pollard, A.J. (2004) *Imagining Robin Hood*, Abingdon: Routledge

Potter, Lois (ed.) (1998) *Playing Robin Hood: The Legend as Performance in Five Centuries*, Newark: University of Delaware Press

Pyle, Howard (1946) *The Merry Adventures of Robin Hood of Great Renown in Nottinghamshire*, New York: Charles Scribner's Sons

Ritson, Joseph (1972) *Robin Hood: A Collection of all the Ancient Poems, Songs, and Ballads*, Wakefield: EP Publishing

Rutherford-Moore, Richard (1998) *The Legend of Robin Hood,* Chievely: Capall Bann Publishing

Walker, J.W. (1973) *The True History of Robin Hood*, Wakefield: E.P. Publishing

INDEX